# New case studies of openness in and beyond the language classroom

Edited by Anna Comas-Quinn,
Ana Beaven, and Barbara Sawhill

Published by Research-publishing.net, a not-for-profit association
Voillans, France, info@research-publishing.net

© 2019 by Editors (collective work)
© 2019 by Authors (individual work)

**New case studies of openness in and beyond the language classroom**
**Edited by Anna Comas-Quinn, Ana Beaven, and Barbara Sawhill**

Publication date: 2019/07/26

**Rights**: the whole volume is published under the Attribution-NonCommercial-NoDerivatives International (CC BY-NC-ND) licence; **individual articles may have a different licence**. Under the CC BY-NC-ND licence, the volume is freely available online (https://doi.org/10.14705/rpnet.2019.37.9782490057511) for anybody to read, download, copy, and redistribute provided that the author(s), editorial team, and publisher are properly cited. Commercial use and derivative works are, however, not permitted.

**Disclaimer**: Research-publishing.net does not take any responsibility for the content of the pages written by the authors of this book. The authors have recognised that the work described was not published before, or that it was not under consideration for publication elsewhere. While the information in this book is believed to be true and accurate on the date of its going to press, neither the editorial team nor the publisher can accept any legal responsibility for any errors or omissions. The publisher makes no warranty, expressed or implied, with respect to the material contained herein. While Research-publishing.net is committed to publishing works of integrity, the words are the authors' alone.

**Trademark notice**: product or corporate names may be trademarks or registered trademarks, and are used only for identification and explanation without intent to infringe.

**Copyrighted material**: every effort has been made by the editorial team to trace copyright holders and to obtain their permission for the use of copyrighted material in this book. In the event of errors or omissions, please notify the publisher of any corrections that will need to be incorporated in future editions of this book.

Typeset by Research-publishing.net
Cover design by © Raphaël Savina (raphael@savina.net)

ISBN13: 978-2-490057-51-1 (Ebook, PDF, colour)
ISBN13: 978-2-490057-52-8 (Ebook, EPUB, colour)
ISBN13: 978-2-490057-50-4 (Paperback - Print on demand, black and white)
Print on demand technology is a high-quality, innovative and ecological printing method; with which the book is never 'out of stock' or 'out of print'.

British Library Cataloguing-in-Publication Data.
A cataloguing record for this book is available from the British Library.

**Legal deposit, UK**: British Library.
**Legal deposit, France**: Bibliothèque Nationale de France - Dépôt légal: juillet 2019.

# Table of contents

v    Notes on contributors

xvii  Foreword
     *Carl S. Blyth*

1    Introduction to new case studies of openness in and beyond the language classroom
     *Anna Comas-Quinn, Ana Beaven, and Barbara Sawhill*

## Section 1. Creating and using OERs

11   An inclusionary open access textbook for Portuguese
     *Carlos Pio and Eduardo Viana da Silva*

23   Creating and implementing open educational resources for the Spanish as a Heritage Language classroom
     *Evelyn Durán Urrea and Jocelly G. Meiners*

37   Italian Open Education: virtual reality immersions for the language classroom
     *Margherita Berti*

49   Embedding OERs for the development of information literacy in the foreign language classroom
     *Odette Gabaudan and Susanna Nocchi*

65   Learning in the open: integrating language and culture through student curation, virtual exchange, and OER
     *Lionel Mathieu, Kathryn Murphy-Judy, Robert Godwin-Jones, Laura Middlebrooks, and Natalia Boykova*

## Section 2. Working in open spaces

85   Building bridges not walls – Wikipedia in Translation Studies
     *Ewan McAndrew and Lorna Campbell*

# Table of contents

- **101**   Working with online communities: translating TED Talks
  *Anna Comas-Quinn and Mara Fuertes Gutiérrez*

- **115**   Repurposing MOOCs for self-regulated language learning in an English for academic purposes course
  *Barbara Conde Gafaro*

- **129**   Assessing language student interaction and engagement via Twitter
  *Olivia Kelly*

- **145**   'Your language development': harnessing openness to integrate independent language learning into the curriculum
  *Tita Beaven*

## Section 3. Openness and teacher development

- **159**   Open practices as a catalyst for language teachers' professional development
  *Patricia Daniels*

- **173**   Empowering teachers and learners in and beyond classrooms: focus on OEPs in reading activities
  *Fanny Meunier, Alice Meurice, and Julie Van de Vyver*

- **187**   Exploratory practice: a way of opening up access to research by classroom teachers and learners
  *Assia Slimani-Rolls*

- **199**   Author index

# Notes on contributors

## 1. Editors

**Anna Comas-Quinn** is Senior Lecturer at the School of Languages and Applied Linguistics at The Open University, UK. She has published on technology enhanced and mobile language learning, teacher development, and open educational resources and practices, and co-edited the first book on open practice in language teaching, Case Studies of Openness in the Language Classroom. Her current research examines the potential of using open online volunteer communities and projects in the teaching of languages and translation.

**Ana Beaven** teaches English as a Foreign Language at the University of Bologna Language Centre. She obtained a PhD in Applied Linguistics from the University of Warwick. Her main fields of interest are foreign language teaching and learning, the use of technology in language teaching, open educational resources and practices, and intercultural education. She co-edited the first volume of Case Studies of Openness in the Language Classroom, and has been involved in various European projects, including WebCEF, CEFcult, and IEREST, which she coordinated. She is presently involved in the RICH-Ed project and the SAREP (Study Abroad Research in European Perspective) COST Action.

**Barbara Sawhill** is Lecturer in Spanish in the Department of Romance Languages and Literatures at Bowdoin College (US). In addition to her teaching practise, she is also the Spanish Language Education Coordinator for the NPR distributed Spanish language podcast Radio Ambulante (http://radioambulante.org). In this role, she works with teachers from around the world to create open educational resource materials to accompany the podcast for use in the classroom. She was delighted to be a part of this second edition of case studies and to work with her fellow co-editors, Ana and Anna. Barbara not-so-secretly hopes they will be able to have the opportunity to do this again in a few years. Barbara's research interests include language pedagogy, task-based learning and teaching listening. She writes about her teaching practise here: http://languagelabunleashed.org.

Notes on contributors

## 2. Reviewers

**Claudia Borghetti** is Research Fellow in Language Learning and Teaching at the Department of Modern Languages, Literature and Cultures, University of Bologna, Italy. She holds an MA in language and intercultural learning through telecollaboration from the University of Bologna, and a PhD in foreign language teaching from the National University of Ireland, Galway. From 2012 to 2015, she was the project manager of the IEREST Project (Intercultural Education Resources for Erasmus Students and their Teachers, LLP 2007-2012, http://www.ierest-project.eu/). She also participated in the Erasmus+ project on multilingualism and interculturality ATIAH (Approaches and Tools for Innovative 'Internationalisation At Home', https://research.ncl.ac.uk/atiah/). She is member of the Management Committee of the COST Action SAREP, http://www.cost.eu/COST_Actions/ca/CA15130). Claudia researches on intercultural language learning and teaching, teaching Italian as a foreign/second language, language socialisation abroad, language learning and teaching in a sociocultural perspective, and (academic) writing.

**Kate Borthwick** is Principal Enterprise Fellow (TEL) in Modern Languages and Linguistics and Director of Programme Development (online education) in the University's Digital Learning team, at the University of Southampton. She leads the University's MOOC programme and has been the course designer on a number of MOOCs. She has extensive experience in online course/materials design and tutoring. She has devised and managed a range of projects exploring open educational practice, the use of open educational resources by language teachers, and the development of open educational resource repositories. She also teaches on PG programmes related to TEL in Modern Languages.

**Todd Bryant** is the Language Technology Specialist at Dickinson College and one of COERLL's "Voices for Openness". He is the creator of the Merlot Classics Award winning open source website "The Mixxer", www.language-exchanges.org, which allows language teachers and students to find partners for language exchanges via Skype. Todd also teaches occasionally in the German department and has written about his experience using social software and games. You can find him on Twitter @bryantt and @MixxerSite.

**Regine Hampel** is Professor of Open and Distance Language Learning at the Open University, UK, and Associate Dean (Research Excellence) in the Faculty of Wellbeing, Education, and Language Studies. Her research explores the impact of using new technologies for language learning and teaching, focussing on the affordances of digital media, task design, learner interaction and communication, online literacies, and teacher training. This has resulted in articles, book chapters, conference presentations, keynotes, special journal issues, and several books, including a forthcoming monograph on 'The disruptive effect of technology on communication and meaning-making in the language classroom: a complex systems theory approach'.

**Kan Qian** is Senior Lecturer in the School of Languages and Applied Linguistics at The Open University (UK) and a Senior Fellow of the British Higher Education Academy. Her research focusses on the use of technologies for the learning and teaching of languages: interactions in online discussion forums, mobile language learning and application design, eTandem learning, and language MOOC design.

**Teresa MacKinnon** is an open practitioner, award winning language teacher, and Certified Member of the Association for Learning Technology. She is experienced in technology enhanced learning design in language education and openly curates professional development resources for language tutors. She researches and designs to find solutions supporting student-centred pedagogy. A career long exponent of the importance of high quality language teaching in the UK, she campaigns for open access to language learning opportunities for all. Teresa is Chair of the Open Education Special Interest Group, which advocates for open educational practices. The group's mission is to support, develop, sustain, and influence policy in open education. Teresa's website (https://sites.google.com/site/lamodification/home); Teresa's social networks (http://about.me/teresamackinnon).

Notes on contributors

**Elena Martín Monje** is Lecturer at UNED (Spain), where she teaches mainly in the areas of English for specific purposes and computer assisted language learning, also her fields of research as a member of ATLAS (Applying Technology to LAnguageS). Both her research and teaching practice have received official recognition, with a prize for Doctoral Excellence at UNED and a University Excellence in Teaching Award. Author of numerous papers in national and international journals, two of her most prominent publications are Language MOOCs: Providing Learning, Transcending Boundaries (2014), which is the first published book on language MOOCs, and the Routledge monographic volume Technology Enhanced Language Learning for Specialised Domains (2016).

**Dr Robert Martínez-Carrasco** is a practising legal translator and part-time Lecturer at Universitat Jaume I (UJI) and Universitat de València (UVEG), where he teaches Inverse Translation (Catalan into English and English linguistics). MA in Legal Translation (City University London), he is a member of the legal translation branch of the GENTT Research Group. His research interests include legal translation education and pedagogy, epistemological bases of education, and curriculum development.

**Fernando Rosell-Aguilar** is Senior Lecturer in Spanish and Open Media Fellow at the School of Languages and Applied Linguistics at the Open University, United Kingdom. He is also Senior Fellow of the Higher Education Academy. He holds an MA in Online and Distance Learning from The Open University. His research focusses on online language learning, mainly the use of apps, Twitter, and podcasting as teaching and learning tools. Other research interests include the use of multimodal synchronous computer mediated communication and task design. He previously taught Spanish at the University of Southampton and the University of Buckingham.

**Pete Smith** is Chief Analytics Officer and Professor of Modern Languages, at the University of Texas at Arlington. His teaching and research focus on big data in education, natural language processing, and natural language understanding, as well as localisation and translation. He also teaches actively in the area of machine translation, including industry partnerships with leading Silicon Valley AI companies into UTA classes and students' learning. Additionally, he oversees UTA's localisation and translation programme, offered to students of seven languages as an introduction to translation and the localisation industry.

**Sarah Sweeney** is the Project Coordinator at the Centre for Open Educational Resources and Language Learning at the University of Texas at Austin, where she works with faculty and high school teachers to develop and promote open educational resources for language learning. She recently led the development of a set of online modules to introduce language instructors to the basic concepts of open educational resources. She has a Masters in Global Communications from the American University of Paris.

**Sylvia Warnecke** holds the post of Staff Tutor Languages at The Open University, UK. She is an experienced tutor and designer of educational offerings, open as well as institutional. She has undertaken a wide range of scholarships and research in the field of online learning and teaching in distance as well as blended contexts. Her work focusses on identity, participation, facilitation, and task design regarding the use of technologies for the learning and teaching of languages and cultures.

## 3. Invited author

**Carl S. Blyth** (PhD, Cornell University) is Associate Professor of French and Director of the Center of Open Educational Resources and Language Learning (COERLL) at the University of Texas at Austin (US). His research focusses on L2 pragmatics, open education, and semiotic approaches to language learning. He has authored several books and book chapters as well as articles in the Modern Language Journal, L2 Journal, CALICO Journal, Journal of Educational Computing Research, ALSIC Revue, and Language & Dialogue. In addition, he has been deeply involved in the development of open educational resources.

Notes on contributors

## 4. Authors

**Tita Beaven** is Senior Lecturer in Spanish in the School of Languages and Applied Linguistics at The Open University. She has a Doctorate in Education in Educational Technology from The Open University and is Senior Fellow of the Higher Education Academy. Her research is in the area of innovative pedagogies and open education, in particular, open educational resources and open educational practices.

**Margherita Berti** is Doctoral Student in Second Language Acquisition and Teaching at the University of Arizona and holds a Master's degree in Linguistics/TESL from Indiana State University. Her current research focusses on the development of openly licensed materials for language assessment and pedagogy with the integration of technology.

**Natalia Boykova** is Assistant Professor of Russian in the VCU School of World Studies. She is native of Moscow, Russia, and a graduate of Moscow Linguistic University. She has more than 25 years of teaching experience in Russia and in the US. She has been teaching at VCU since 2005, where she teaches all levels of undergraduate education. She coordinates the Russian programme. She has been an active member of the Curation, Virtual Exchange, and OER Project since its beginning.

**Lorna Campbell** works for the University of Edinburgh's OER Service, where her work includes strategies for embedding and supporting open education and OER within the institution. She is Trustee of Wikimedia UK and has 20 years' experience working in education technology and open education policy and practice.

**Barbara Conde Gafaro** (BA, PGDip, MA) completed her MA in ELT and Applied Linguistics with a dissertation on a blended MOOC integration at Coventry University. She is currently studying for her PhD on MOOCs for Foreign Language Learning at the Open University, supported by the award of a Leverhulme scholarship.

# Notes on contributors

**Patricia Daniels** is a freelance English language teacher who has taught in diverse contexts in Switzerland since 1992. She is currently working towards her Doctorate in Education (EdD) at The Open University (UK). Her research interests include open educational resources, open educational practices, and professional development.

**Evelyn Durán Urrea** is Lecturer in the Department of Languages and Literatures at Lehman College. She holds an MA in Hispanic Linguistics from the University of Arizona and a PhD from the Pennsylvania State University; her research interests include bilingualism, Spanish-English code-switching, and Spanish as a heritage language. Her research has focussed on assessment and placement of heritage and second language learners of Spanish at the college level, practices in the foreign language classroom; specifically, a pedagogical model for the learning of Spanish as a heritage language based on the flipped classroom approach and open educational resources initiatives.

**Mara Fuertes Gutiérrez** is Lecturer in Spanish and the Head of Spanish at the School of Languages and Applied Linguistics at The Open University, UK. Mara's fields of expertise are linguistics and Spanish and over her career she has conducted extensive research, published works, and lead research projects in the areas of teaching and learning Spanish as a foreign language, historiography of linguistics, linguistic typology, and sociolinguistics.

**Odette Gabaudan** is Lecturer in French at Technological University Dublin. Her research interest is in e-learning and in particular the integration of technology in her language teaching. She has co-produced a number of OERs for foreign language learning including frenchgrammartour.com and digilanguages.ie.

**Robert Godwin-Jones** is Professor, School of World Studies. His research is in applied linguistics, with an emphasis on language learning and technology and intercultural communication. He writes a regular column for the journal Language Learning & Technology on emerging technologies.

Notes on contributors

**Olivia Kelly** has been working as Associate Lecturer with The Open University since 2007, teaching on a variety of communication and language courses. She is Senior Fellow of the Higher Education Academy, experienced in developing online teaching materials and in teaching and enhancing study skills for students at HE level, and also works as a consultant writer of educational materials. She holds an Honours degree in European Regional Development and a Masters degree in Social Sciences. She has always had a keen interest in how students interact in online spaces, having completed research into student interactions on course VLE forums, and is now particularly interested in how open social media resources such as Twitter enhance or change that student interaction.

**Lionel Mathieu**, is Lecturer in French in the Department of Romance Studies at Boston University (Fall 2018). A native of Strasbourg, France, he has his PhD in linguistics from the University of Arizona, with a concentration in second language acquisition and teaching. He has been an active member of the Curation, Virtual Exchange, and OER Project since its inception in 2015 at Virginia Commonwealth University.

**Ewan McAndrew** is Wikimedian in Residence at the University of Edinburgh supporting the university's commitment to sharing open knowledge and developing information literacy and digital skills since 2016. Prior to this, Ewan has worked as an English and Media teacher in Japan, Singapore, South Korea, and in Scotland.

**Jocelly G. Meiners** is Lecturer in the Department of Spanish and Portuguese at the University of Texas at Austin, where she teaches Heritage Spanish courses. She holds a PhD in Hispanic Linguistics from the University of Texas at Austin, and an MA in French Linguistics. Her research interests include pragmatics and emotion in second language acquisition, heritage Spanish learners and pedagogy, as well as linguistic attitudes and language maintenance regarding Spanish in the US. Jocelly serves as co-project Director for the Texas Coalition for Heritage Spanish (TeCHS), hosted by COERLL.

**Fanny Meunier** is Professor of English language, linguistics, and didactics at UCLouvain, Belgium. She has been involved in learner corpus research for over 25 years and her main research interest is the link between second language acquisition studies and pedagogical applications. She is also actively involved in pre- and in-service teacher training and is collaborating with several international research projects on, among other aspects, bi- and multi-literacies and digital literacies.

**Alice Meurice** is research Assistant in modern language didactics and English for specific purposes Teacher at UCLouvain (Belgium). Her main research area is foreign language teaching and, more specifically, the integration of information and communication technologies in the foreign language learning classroom and curriculum. Other research interests include the use of OERs in language learning in primary and secondary education.

**Laura Middlebrooks** is Assistant Professor of Spanish and Coordinator of Languages, School of World Studies. She holds an MA degree in Latin American Studies from the University of New Mexico. She earned a second MA in Romance Languages from the University of Pennsylvania. At Boston University she wrote her PhD dissertation on the sexual rhetoric of translation in the works of Rosario Ferré and Esmeralda Santiago. She joined VCU in 2008 and has taught linguistics, history of the Spanish language, translation, interpretation, and all levels of grammar.

**Kathryn Murphy-Judy** is Associate Professor of French and Coordinator of Languages in the VCU School of World Studies. She works in technology enhanced language instruction, with work spanning video and videodiscs, to multimedia production, to online language teaching and learning, and now this highly collaborative, interactive, open educational resource design, development, and deployment project.

**Susanna Nocchi** is Lecturer in Italian at Technological University Dublin. Her research interests lie in computer assisted language learning, particularly in the

## Notes on contributors

application of activity theory and sociocultural learning theories to the study of e-learning environments. Her most recent research focusses on the development of digital literacies and multimedia translation for FL learning. She has been working in the field of Italian as an FL as a teacher, author, and researcher. She has participated in the digilanguages.ie project.

**Carlos Pio** is Lecturer in Foreign Languages at the University of Pennsylvania, in Philadelphia, United States. He completed his PhD in Hispanic Languages and Literature with an emphasis in European Medieval Studies at the University of California, Santa Barbara. He has been teaching Portuguese, literature, and cinema from Portugal, Africa, and Brazil, Portuguese for the professions, and Spanish. In 2019, he received the Penn Arts & Sciences Language Teaching Innovation Grant for the development of an inclusionary e-textbook for Portuguese in Guinea-Bissau.

**Assia Slimani-Rolls** is Reader of Applied Linguistics and Education and Head of Research and Professional Development in the Institute of Languages and Culture at Regent's University, London. Her research interests include exploratory practice (a form of practitioner research), language learning, language teacher education, teacher professional identity, and continuing professional development. Her belief in the collaborative work by teachers and learners to understand better their classroom practice has been heightened further since working with language teachers and learners on several projects to implement exploratory practice in their classroom, which led to her latest co-authored publication *Exploratory Practice for continuing professional development – an innovative approach for language teachers*.

**Julie Van de Vyver** is PhD Student and Teaching Assistant in English linguistics and didactics at UCLouvain, Belgium. Her main research area is foreign language teaching and, more specifically, the integration of mobile technologies in the foreign language learning classroom and curriculum. Other research interests include the use of OERs on language learning in secondary education.

**Eduardo Viana da Silva** is the Portuguese Programme Coordinator at the University of Washington (UW) in Seattle, US. He has received his PhD in Hispanic Studies with an emphasis in Applied Linguistics from the University of California, Santa Barbara (UCSB). Eduardo also holds an interdisciplinary degree in teaching "Certificate in College and University Teaching" from UCSB. His main areas of interest are applied linguistics, teaching languages for specific purposes, Luso-Brazilian literature and culture, and curriculum development with a focus on the use of technology, culture, and task-based language teaching. He has received the UW Libraries Open Textbook Award for the development of an open e-text for first year Portuguese classes.

# Foreword

## Carl S. Blyth[1]

Today, in the field of foreign language teaching, there is much talk of shifting paradigms. The term *paradigm* was popularized by the American physicist Thomas Kuhn in his 1962 book entitled *The Structure of Scientific Revolutions*. According to Kuhn, scientific progress is neither linear nor continuous, but rather subject to abrupt shifts in the consensus of a scientific community. To illustrate this phenomenon, Kuhn cites the well-known shift in astronomy from *geocentrism* (the belief that the sun and the planets revolve around the Earth) to *heliocentrism* (the belief that the Earth and the planets revolve around the sun). Kuhn stresses that paradigms are defined by contrasting concepts and discourses and, as a result, are largely incommensurable. Kuhn also notes that paradigm shifts are not only a matter of accepting new facts, but of reorganizing those facts into a new worldview. In other words, paradigm shifts entail objective as well as subjective change.

Despite examples of revolutionary change in the sciences, paradigm shifts in the humanities – such as in foreign language education – appear to be more gradual. Most foreign language educators integrate new ideas into their curricular and pedagogical practices in an incremental process of professional development. Personally, I believe that paradigm change in foreign language teaching is largely a matter of educators learning by example from each other. Simply put, there is nothing more powerful than a case study for catalyzing change in our field. And in this book, *New case studies of openness in and beyond the language classroom*, foreign language specialists share their stories of personal and professional transformation in the well-known form of a case study. Following the same format, each case study provides the reader with the necessary information to understand and to implement a specific pedagogical or curricular innovation. For

1. Director, Center for Open Educational Resources and Language Learning, University of Texas at Austin, United States; cblyth@austin.utexas.edu

**How to cite:** Blyth, C. S. (2019). Foreword. In A. Comas-Quinn, A. Beaven & B. Sawhill (Eds), *New case studies of openness in and beyond the language classroom* (pp. xvii-xviii). Research-publishing.net. https://doi.org/10.14705/rpnet.2019.37.961

example, each case study includes a detailed description of a new project, the intended student outcomes, as well as the tools and resources used in the project.

While many case studies focus on the use of ready-made Open Educational Resources (OERs), others describe how to integrate Open Educational Practices (OEPs) into foreign language classes. Several case studies explain how to implement principles of open pedagogy such as the creation of a Wikipedia page or a translation of a TED Talk by the students themselves. In such cases, students are challenged to follow the editorial guidelines of Wikipedia and TED for the creation of open content. Thus, in the open language classroom, students share their knowledge with the world while, at the same time, improving their proficiency in the target language. In short, each case study described in this book is a beautiful illustration of the *creative commons in action*. I sincerely hope that foreign language educators who read these case studies will embrace the affordances of openness for themselves and their students and thereby shift the paradigm one classroom at a time.

For an open world.

# Introduction to new case studies of openness in and beyond the language classroom

### Anna Comas-Quinn[1], Ana Beaven[2], and Barbara Sawhill[3]

## 1. The project, six years on

Our previous edited volume, *Case studies of openness in the language classroom* (Beaven, Comas-Quinn, & Sawhill, 2013), was published in 2013 following the EUROCALL conference "Learning through Sharing: Open Resources, Open Practices, Open Communication" held the previous year in Bologna, Italy. At this event, we realised that the innovative work language practitioners were developing in their teaching had to be shared more widely. The edited volume we published showcased some of the ways in which language practitioners were engaging with the concept of openness and aimed to inspire and encourage teachers to experiment further with open resources and open practices. Five years on, we have decided to revisit our project, and to once more check the pulse of openness in and beyond the language classroom. Our purpose has remained unchanged: to give a voice to practitioners themselves, and bring to the surface some of the excellent and innovative work that language teachers and learners are engaged in.

In our previous volume, we took Open Educational Resources (OERs) to mean "materials used to support education that may be freely accessed, reused, modified and shared by anyone" (Downes, 2011, n.p.). UNESCO's (2019) recently agreed definition of OERs continues to emphasise open licensing as the means to make content reusable and shareable:

---

1. The Open University, Milton Keynes, England; anna.comas-quinn@open.ac.uk; https://orcid.org/0000-0002-8290-4315

2. Università di Bologna, Bologna, Italy; ana.beaven@unibo.it; https://orcid.org/0000-0003-3289-3010

3. Bowdoin College, Brunswick, Maine, United States; bsawhill@bowdoin.edu; https://orcid.org/0000-0003-2594-1862

**How to cite:** Comas-Quinn, A., Beaven, A, & Sawhill, B. (2019). Introduction to new case studies of openness in and beyond the language classroom. In A. Comas-Quinn, A. Beaven & B. Sawhill (Eds), *New case studies of openness in and beyond the language classroom* (pp. 1-8). Research-publishing.net. https://doi.org/10.14705/rpnet.2019.37.962

Introduction

> "Open Educational Resources are teaching, learning and research materials in any medium – digital or otherwise – that reside in the public domain or have been released under an open license that permits no-cost access, use, adaptation and redistribution by others with no or limited restrictions" (UNESCO, 2019, n.p.).

There have been many definitions of open practice since our book was published, some more narrowly focussed on the use of OERs, others much broader, taking into account not only open resources but the affordances that openness makes available to teachers and learners (for a full discussion, see Cronin & McLaren, 2018). Weller's (2017) broad definition of open educational practice as "any significant change in educational practice afforded by the open nature of the internet" (n.p.) seems to us a useful starting point for a pedagogy that adopts openness as a mindset and includes "freedom, justice, respect, openness as attitude or culture, the absence of barriers, promotion of sharing, accessibility, transparency, collaboration, agency, self-direction, personalization and ubiquitous ownership" (Baker, 2017, pp. 131-132).

Learners are increasingly accessing free online and open resources, tools, and spaces where they can develop their language skills beyond the classroom, alone, or in collaboration with others, and often whilst engaging in purposeful and enjoyable activities. Examples in the literature can be found for, amongst others, online gaming (Thorne, Black, & Sykes, 2009), fanfiction sites (Sauro, 2017), and mobile language learning apps (Rosell-Aguilar, 2018). Rather than ignore these developments, teachers need to find ways to explore and connect these activities productively with the formal learning that they design for their students, as shown in many of the contributions in this volume.

## 2. Contents and audience

Like the previous volume, this collection is addressed primarily to foreign and second language teachers in secondary and tertiary education. We have maintained the same approach and kept to case studies as a more accessible format for time-pressured educators. Authors were asked to provide sufficient context and detail about their projects to enable other practitioners to replicate or build upon the activities described in each case study. Whilst these are not research papers, the projects here included are often the result of pedagogical research, engagement with open education, and extensive experience of language learning and teaching.

The chapters in this volume have been divided into three sections: creating and using OERs, working in open spaces, and openness and teacher development. The following sections provide an overview of the contents of the book through brief summaries of each case study. We hope this will make it easier for readers to locate those projects that will be more relevant to them.

## 2.1. Creating and using OERs

This section opens with **Pio** and **Viana da Silva**'s description of the creation of an inclusionary open e-textbook for teaching Portuguese. Their understanding of 'openness' does not include only the fact that the textbook is freely available to anyone with access to the Internet, but also the bottom-up approach taken in the writing process, during which Portuguese speakers from different socioeconomic backgrounds in the United States and Brazil provided feedback. Thus, the representation of minority groups, leading for example to the use of masculine, feminine, and non-binary genders, became an integral part of the texbook.

**Durán Urrea** and **Meiners** come together to discuss OERs for a growing community in the United States: heritage learners of Spanish. Standard textbooks and teaching materials do not address the specific needs of students for whom Spanish is their home language but not always their main spoken or written language. The authors introduce a repository of OERs created for and by teachers of heritage Spanish as well as examples of how OERs can be used in a specific course.

**Berti** shares with us the development of an open online repository for storing, sharing and accessing virtual reality videos used as language teaching resources in undergraduate beginner and intermediate Italian courses in the United States. Beyond describing this interesting way of incorporating OERs into Italian language courses, Berti shares suggestions for tools required to create additional videos.

In their action research study **Gabaudan** and **Nocchi** investigated the embedding of selected components of DigiLanguages, an OER for Digital Literacies for Foreign Languages, within a Bachelor of Arts in International Business and Languages at a higher education institution in Ireland. The aim of the two teachers and researchers was to identify affordances and constraints in the introduction and adaptation of a specific resource in their foreign language classroom, and to investigate the potential of the OER to change pedagogical practices in the area of digital literacies for foreign language learning.

In the last chapter of this initial section, **Mathieu**, **Murphy-Judy**, **Godwin-Jones**, **Middlebrooks**, and **Boykova** discuss a well-developed project consisting of a four-stage process and OER platform. Students are directly involved in curating authentic materials, creating interactive modules, developing interactive virtual exchanges with native speakers and finally creating OERs that exemplify communicative activities and which eventually become sustainable, relevant, and student-driven resources for language learning.

## 2.2. Working in open spaces

In the opening chapter to this section, **McAndrew** and **Campbell** describe a translation project for postgraduate translation students using Wikipedia. Students complete the translation of a Wikipedia article using Wikipedia's Content Translation tool, which enables them to focus on creating a high-quality translation without needing to worry about formatting issues. Through this, students obtain experience publishing their translation as a transition between their university education and the world of work.

Similarly, **Comas-Quinn** and **Fuertes Gutiérrez** illustrate their use of TED Translators, a project in which volunteers translate the subtitles of TED Talks, to introduce translation and subtitling to advanced language students. In spite of the technical challenge and the unpredictability of working in an open community, participants found this activity enjoyable and appreciated the freedom to choose what they wanted to translate as well as the support provided by other students through peer reviews of their translation.

**Conde Gafaro** investigates the self-regulated learning strategies – in terms of goal setting, planning, monitoring, and adjusting strategies – that university students employ whilst engaging with Massive Open Online Courses (MOOCs) as part of an English for Academic Purposes course. She suggests that using MOOCs as supplementary material during a face-to-face academic English course can have positive effects on learning and boost self-regulation.

Twitter is the focus of **Kelly**'s case study. She explores this accessible environment for student interaction and engagement through a virtual ethnographic analysis of the tweets of language students in a distance education course. A sentiment analysis of the words used in the tweets reveals a generally positive feeling regarding their studies and the support provided by their teachers and peers.

**Beaven** outlines how open practices and tools are used in a postgraduate translation qualification. Students diagnose their own language development needs whilst learning about the open tools, resources, strategies, and learning communities available to the translating community. Students are introduced to ways of developing their language skills in both their main and other languages, whilst at the same time becoming aware of the key role of language development in their ongoing professional development as translators.

## 2.3. Openness and teacher development

**Daniels** opens this section with a small-scale pilot study that sheds light on the open educational practices of freelance English language teachers in Switzerland within their continuing professional development. The author looks at open teaching practices and digital networking practices, and concludes that these open practices can lead to improved digital literacy as well as literacy and language skills.

Introduction

**Meunier, Meurice**, and **Van de Vyver**'s case study is set within a broader Belgian government project dedicated to language learning and teaching, and explores reading strategies outside the classroom for Dutch as a foreign language using a mobile hunt in the Hergé Museum (Louvain-la-Neuve, Belgium). The participants involved are pre-service teachers and primary-school pupils learning Dutch. The author discusses mobile and classroom open educational practices, the development of in-service teachers' and learners' digital literacy skills, and the creation of professional learning communities.

In the closing chapter, **Slimani-Rolls** discusses the potentially transformative impact of practitioner research, and more specifically exploratory practice, on the professional development of language teachers. Through a case study that looks at how a teacher addressed the issue of disruptive mobile-phone use in her classrooms, the author exemplifies this type of scholarship and urges teachers to engage in and make their research public, thus contributing to their own professional development as well as that of colleagues globally.

## 3.  Final thoughts

We are grateful to the authors who shared their case studies with us, and by extension, with you, our readers. In an academic world that is becoming increasingly limited by costly textbooks and online paywalls, we are delighted to help celebrate the open and accessible work of our colleagues across the globe, and the opportunity this openness creates to learn from one another. We hope you will find, as did we, these case studies to be inspiring examples of best practice in open language learning and teaching, in and beyond the classroom.

## Acknowledgements

We are grateful to Research-publishing.net, and in particular to Sylvie Thouësny, for supporting us in this endeavour and for providing, through their Give Back campaign, the means through which these works can be shared openly with the teaching community.

The editors would like to express their profound appreciation for the work of the peer reviewers. In keeping with the theme of openness, we chose to utilise an open peer review system when evaluating the manuscripts. Reviewers knew the names of the authors and as a result, we found, the comments and questions received by the reviewers were honest and respectful of the work being done by their colleagues. These reviewers provided us with invaluable commentaries about the content, the tone, the utility, and the clarity of the works for which the editors are extremely grateful. The peer reviewers were (in alphabetical order): Claudia Borghetti, Kate Borthwick, Todd Bryant, Regine Hampel, Kan Qian, Teresa MacKinnon, Elena Martín Monje, Robert Martínez-Carrasco, Fernando Rosell-Aguilar, Pete Smith, Sarah Sweeney, and Sylvia Warnecke.

Finally, the editors would like to thank their friends and families for their patience and support as we worked to bring this volume to completion. It has been an honour to have the opportunity to work as a team of editors again and we truly hope you enjoy this book as much as we enjoyed working with one another and with the authors to make it happen.

## References

Baker, F. W. (2017). An alternative approach: openness in education over the last 100 years. *TechTrends, 61*(2), 130-140. https://doi.org/10.1007/s11528-016-0095-7

Beaven, A., Comas-Quinn, A., & Sawhill, B. (Eds). (2013). *Case studies of openness in the language classroom*. Research-publishing.net. https://doi.org/10.14705/rpnet.2013.9781908416100

Cronin, C., & McLaren, I. (2018). Conceptualising OEP: a review of theoretical and empirical literature in open educational practices. *Open Praxis, 10*(2), 127-143. https://doi.org/10.5944/openpraxis.10.2.825

Downes, S. (2011, July 14). *Open educational resources: a definition*. http://www.downes.ca/archive/11/07_18_news_OLDaily.htm

## Introduction

Rosell-Aguilar, F. (2018). Autonomous language learning through a mobile application: a user evaluation of the busuu app. *Computer Assisted Language Learning, 31*(8), 854-881. https://doi.org/10.1080/09588221.2018.1456465

Sauro, S. (2017). Online fan practices and CALL. *CALICO Journal, 34*(2), 131-46.

Thorne, S. L., Black, R. W., & Sykes, J. (2009). Second language use, socialization, and learning in internet interest communities and online gaming. *The Modern Language Journal, 93*(s1), 802-821. https://doi.org/10.1111/j.1540-4781.2009.00974.x

UNESCO (2019). *Open Educational Resources (OER)*. https://en.unesco.org/themes/building-knowledge-societies/oer

Weller, M. (2017, April 12). *My definition is this.* http://blog.edtechie.net/oep/my-definition-is-this/

# Section 1.
# Creating and using OERs

# 1. An inclusionary open access textbook for Portuguese

### Carlos Pio[1] and Eduardo Viana da Silva[2]

## Abstract

This case study describes the development of an e-textbook for first-year Portuguese classes. This pedagogical initiative strives to provide an inclusionary and open textbook for Portuguese, including the collaboration and feedback from Portuguese speakers of several economic and cultural backgrounds. In this context, 'openness' means listening to the language of a given community and the commitment to reproduce it in a textbook format. Inclusion of minority groups in the textbook is perceived not as 'curiosities', but as an integral part of the cultures being represented so that a wider range of communities and language registers (from formal to informal) is portrayed. In addition, openness applies to the articulation of gender narratives in an inclusionary format. For instance, the masculine gender is supplemented with female and other non-binary genders. Above all, this textbook is adaptive and open to all, regardless of economic background. By promoting language teaching and quality free education to all, it is our intention to contribute to a better understanding of each other and to the reduction of the divisions among communities. In this project, the authors decided to create materials in an open platform (Creative Commons CC BY), available to any student with access to the Internet. In order to be inclusive, the authors worked in partnership with language professionals and students from several institutions in the US and in Brazil. Through a collaborative effort, the authors produced an inclusive e-textbook created from the bottom up.

1. University of Pennsylvania, Philadelphia, Pennsylvania, United States; bcarlos@upenn.edu

2. University of Washington, Seattle, Washington, United States; evsilva@uw.edu

**How to cite this chapter:** Pio, C., & Viana da Silva, E. (2019). An inclusionary open access textbook for Portuguese. In A. Comas-Quinn, A. Beaven & B. Sawhill (Eds), *New case studies of openness in and beyond the language classroom* (pp. 11-22). Research-publishing.net. https://doi.org/10.14705/rpnet.2019.37.963

Chapter 1

**Keywords: Portuguese, e-textbook, textbook, open educational resource, diversity, inclusion, LGBTQI.**

## 1.  Context of the project

The curriculum of Portuguese as an additional language has been dominated by a few textbooks, most of them published in Brazil, Portugal, and the US. In general, the textbooks are expensive and in the case of the US, the market is controlled mainly by one publishing house which charges a fee for temporary access to the online workbook, substantially raising the costs to students. Given the limited demand for Portuguese – it corresponds to less than 1% of the foreign languages taught in the US (Looney & Lusin, 2018[3]) – publishing houses tend to limit the publication of new textbook editions, which is visible in the outdated material.

According to our experience, introductory language books for Portuguese are mostly written by language specialists who do not teach introductory level classes. In the end, most of the activities in the textbooks have not been tested with students before, and sometimes do not work in a class setting. Finally, language textbooks printed outside Portuguese-speaking countries are written by language professionals who generally have not been in contact with everyday and current Portuguese for many years, which is noticeable in the word-choices and the outdated usage of language expressions. The writing process of printed textbooks for Portuguese follows a top-down approach, which limits the representation of cultural aspects to those experienced by the authors. It is not uncommon to sense a unifying cultural voice throughout a language textbook, instead of multiple voices. The representation of minority groups is often left to readings and blurbs instead of being an integral part of the material (for a discussion on the underrepresentation of minorities in English textbooks, including women, people of colour, low-income people, and the disabled, see Hilliard, 2014; Kubota, Austin, & Saito-Abbott, 2003).

---

3. In the 2016 Modern Language Association of America report, Portuguese corresponds to 0.69% of the enrollments in foreign languages in institutions of higher education in the US.

The idea of developing an open e-textbook for Portuguese grew from the experience of the authors who have taught entry-language classes at university level for over 15 years each. Having developed several class activities over the years tailored to their classes and having to adapt most of the textbooks' content in order to provide a more natural usage of Portuguese, the authors decided to work with colleagues and students in order to create an open e-textbook. The goal of this project is to provide language learners with an e-textbook that is current, free of charge, and available to anyone with access to the Internet. This material is tailored to university students, however, most of the book could also work with high school students and with adults in general. Furthermore, this e-textbook is also a tool for other Portuguese language teachers. The development of this material is a collective effort. It involves the participation of several language students and Portuguese instructors in Brazil, the United States, and Portugal (and in the future, Portuguese-speaking countries in Africa). Most of the writing has been done in Brazil and Portugal, taking into consideration the result of surveys with students and instructors. Overall, the material reflects several voices and gives prominence to minority groups and gender equality throughout the text, including the representation of the Lesbian, Gay, Bisexual, Transgender, Questioning, and Intersex (LGBTQI) community and other disenfranchised groups, such as immigrants in Brazil and Portugal, for example.

## 2. Intended outcomes

Current Portuguese as a foreign language books do not offer a sufficient range of real language, despite the fact that they make an effort in taking the language outside the classroom and making it more real. There is the need to take a step further by presenting everyday language spoken by Portuguese speakers from several backgrounds. This real use of language is a learning outcome that many instructors struggle to achieve in their classrooms. Realness and openness occur when listening to the language in use in a given community, taking into consideration all of its sociological variables such as economic standing, ethnicity, origins and citizenship, and the willingness to reproduce such language in the textbook format (Pérez-Leroux & Glass, 2000). To include these variables entails a shift in paradigm from teaching and learning languages believing that only a speaker who speaks really 'well' a language can produce meaningful input versus believing that any speaker can produce meaningful input acknowledging the effectiveness of their message according to a specific social situation (Mendonça, 2012). In other words, the input in Portuguese produced by a speaker in a *musseque* (slum) in Luanda is as valid as the input in Portuguese produced by a speaker brought up in the middle class, holding a university degree in Lisbon, or by a speaker who speaks Uruguayan Portuguese on the border between Brazil and Uruguay. All of them should be included in the classroom so that students understand why and how they can use the target language and what to do with it.

The inclusion of minority groups in the textbook is then to be perceived not as 'curiosities' but as an integral part of the country being represented so that a wider range of communities and language registers (from formal to informal) is exemplified. Also, openness applies to the articulation of gender narratives in an inclusionary format. In Portuguese, gender is expressed through two classic forms, -a for feminine and -o for masculine. So both should be alternated with non-binary grammatical uses (namely *tod@s, todxs, tod_s, todos, todas*).

In regards to technological tools, discussion boards, such as the ones on Blackboard, Canvas, and Moodle, are a great tool for addressing complex concepts in a language class, like the definition of ethnicity, colour, citizenship, gender, and sexuality. A Romani student may encounter difficulties in a classroom whose majority is non-Romani, so a blog functions as a safe stress-free environment for that student or any other to choose or express her/his origins. Also, the definition – and even the explanation – in the classroom of a group other than the majority may cause confrontation and anxiety, so an educational blog is a less heated environment for a larger discussion, rather than utilising standard definitions given by a 'normal' or 'classic' discourse of a language and a culture which leaves out everyday important and real expressions of the self.

Another outcome in this project is the application of inclusive language. When dealing with race, the classic explanation of Black culture in Portuguese-speaking countries is given by saying that *preto* and *negro* refer to the same colour, but *negro* should be used for Afro-Brazilians or Afro-Portuguese and *preto* for objects. Nonetheless, what do instructors say to students when their Brazilian and Portuguese friends do not call themselves *negro* but *preto* and when the characters of the videos, movies, and documentaries they watch address their African origins using words such as *caboclx*, *negrx*, *pretx*, *morenx*, *morenx clarx*, or *cafusx* to express their different shades of blackness? An inclusive material should provide other words besides *negro* and *preto* so that an African descendant student can express her/his identity in the target language more properly (and, more importantly, as one chooses to). This concept applies as well for a lesbian student, for example, who chooses to reveal her sexual preferences or identity not in a classroom but rather in a blog.

Finally, language textbooks frequently create a deceiving narrative of inclusion and equality. The perpetuation of a single voice throughout language textbooks, the voice of privileged writers, is many times confused with false ideas of equality. The authors of the Portuguese textbook – *Bate Papo* – strongly believe that in order to include authentic perspectives of minorities in textbooks, the members of the minority groups should participate as collaborators in the creation of the teaching material. There is an eminent risk of creating clichés and reinforcing stereotypes when a textbook author creates the 'voices' of minorities without being a part of the given minority group.

## 3. Nuts and bolts

This Portuguese textbook *Bate Papo* was created as an electronic text with a Creative Commons license (CC BY), which allows anyone to share and adapt the material as long as the appropriate credit is given. The textbook is available online, on Word, and on PDF as well, so students can print it at home. Since it is an electronic textbook, the authors are able to make changes and review the material on a regular basis, keeping it up-to-date, reflecting the changes in the language, and including current cultural manifestations as well. The text is available through the PressBooks platform from the University of Washington: https://uw.pressbooks.pub/batepapo/ – which is currently under construction, as the authors are releasing the chapters once they are piloted with their language classes. The selection of images represents the book's intention of being truly inclusive. The sample below from Unit 2, which focusses on physical descriptions, has the image of Marielle Franco (Figure 1), an Afro-Brazilian politician and activist, who was assassinated in 2017.

Figure 1.   Introduction to Unit 2

CC BY Viana da Silva
*Bate-Papo* - Unidade 2- Parte A- vol 1

**Bate-Papo – Unidade 2 – Parte A**

By the end of this lesson, you will be able to:
- List basic colors.
- Describe physical appearances and personalities.
- List some daily and leisure activities.
- Ask simple questions about daily routines.
- List modes of transportation.
- List the months.
- Propose simple plans for the weekends/ future months.

Marielle Franco
Ativista Social e Política carioca

In the same unit about physical descriptions, other images include iconic figures in the Portuguese-speaking world who are not generally portrayed in traditional language textbooks, such as the Afro-Brazilian reporter Glória Maria, the Brazilian iconic transexual, Gilberta Salci Júnior, and the Guiné Bissau politician, Amílcar Cabral (Figure 4). One other activity is the celebration of Afro Lusophone History Month (Figure 2), in which students are asked to search information about individuals who have been important for Black history in the Lusophone world and how they might relate these people's accomplishments to their own cultures (Figure 3). For example, Paulina Chiziane, one of the first women writers from Mozambique; Mamadou Ba, head of the SOS Racism

Association in Portugal; and Brazilian Geanine Escobar, activist for the Black Lesbian Women rights in Portugal.

Figure 2. Cultural activity

Figure 3. Activity prompts

Cultura. Escolha uma destas personalidades e faça uma apresentação em aula sobre:

- quem é ou quem foi,
- por que razões é importante para a cultura do seu país,
- por que razões você escolheu essa personalidade,
- tem outras personalidades no seu país que façam coisas semelhantes?

Figure 4.  Vocabulary for physical descriptions

In addition to the iconography, a series of short videos were produced portraying everyday life from different ethnicities people in Brazil in several situations, such as greeting each other and purchasing an item in a store, for example. Besides the diversity shown in the videos, the material presents a series of Portuguese dialects from several regions of Brazil and from different socioeconomic backgrounds. Since the content of the book is built from the conversation in the dialogues, the language being studied is the language used in everyday Portuguese. The authors worked carefully with the contributors for the videos by giving them the freedom of choosing the words that they would use normally, without a rehearsed transcript. The result is a more natural language. The expressions and language structures introduced in the dialogues are then explained through a Portuguese/English glossary and by focussing on the task at hand, allowing students to complete simple tasks despite the complexity of the language. It was clear to the authors that the conversations recorded on video brought a range of expressions, accents, intonations, language structures, and vocabulary that would not be represented otherwise.

As for the online workbook that accompanies the e-textbook, the exercises are currently available as Creative Commons on the Canvas platform. In the future, the online workbook will also be available on the Moodle and Blackboard platforms. Although this Portuguese e-textbook is innovative and inclusive, the authors recognise the importance of also offering the traditional automated online exercises as language practice, especially at the lower levels of proficiency. The online exercises range from controlled exercises to open ones.

One challenging aspect of the online workbook is the series of exercises that are corrected by the online platforms (Moodle, Canvas, and Blackboard). There are limitations in the correction system due to the capabilities of the technological tools. For instance, when a student misses an accent, the whole answer is considered wrong, despite it being a single accent missing. It will probably be the case that in the future, these online platforms will be more refined and able to detect different kinds of answers and scale the grade according to the number of inaccuracies.

Another aspect that contributed to the development of this e-textbook in Portuguese is the use of other open educational resources, especially the podcasts *Língua da Gente*, produced by Orlando Kelm and available at the Centre for Open Educational Resources and Language Learning at the University of Texas at Austin (https://linguadagente.coerll.utexas.edu/). The podcasts focus on a short dialogue between two Brazilians and are listed according to the level of proficiency being targeted: beginner, elementary, and intermediate. Another important open source is the grammar book *Português para Principiantes* (https://wisc.pb.unizin.org/portuguese/), available through the University of Wisconsin-Madison, on their PressBooks platform. Their grammar explanations were incorporated in *Bate Papo*. At the end, thanks to the open educational resources, *Língua da Gente* and *Português para Principiantes*, the e-textbook *Bate Papo* is richer and more complete. The authors can then focus on interactive class activities and aspects not yet covered or not dealt with well by previous textbooks in Portuguese, such as the inclusion of LGBTQI voices and the representation of indigenous and Afro populations from the Portuguese-speaking world, for example. The reusing and remixing of digital open educational resources works as an advantage to educators who are constantly looking for ways to improve their teaching materials.

Chapter 1

The book *Bate Papo* is designed into two versions. In the first stage, the language focus is on Brazilian Portuguese. All the videos and most of the collaborators in this first version of the book come from Brazil, including professors and students in applied linguistics. In a second and future stage, the book will focus also on European Portuguese. The plan is to reproduce the majority of the content from the Brazilian Portuguese textbook contextualised in an European Portuguese version. The e-textbook will then be offered in two versions: Brazilian Portuguese and European Portuguese. The fact is that Brazilian Portuguese and European Portuguese are linguistically and culturally very different. A third proposal is an African Portuguese version of the textbook, which should come from collaborators in Mozambique and Angola.

Finally, the authors will provide a print-on-demand version of the material on a low-cost option (around USD20) for those who prefer to have the printed material on hand during class time, even though there is the possibility of printing a PDF or Word Copy available online. The collaborators in language schools and higher education institutions in Brazil have already signaled their intentions of adopting this e-textbook. It comes as no surprise that schools with immigrant populations in Brazil find this material very helpful with its grammar explanations and glossaries in English, according to Nildicéia Aparecida Rocha, from the Universidade Estadual Paulista (personal communication, June 21, 2018). Programmes for immigrant students in Brazil have struggled with teaching material that lacks a common language for their target audiences.

In practical terms, to make the e-textbook *Bate Papo* available to a larger audience and to make it truly open will involve massive promotion with Portuguese language instructors, students, universities, colleges, public and private language schools, non-profit organisations, and the social media. The intention of having this e-textbook as an open educational resource is also to give an opportunity to underprivileged students to study Portuguese with a quality material that represents the diversity of the Portuguese-speaking world and which is also free. Since platforms such as Canvas and Blackboard[4] are

---

4. Canvas is a free and open platform, whereas Blackboard charges a fee.

normally used at universities and colleges in the United States, the possibility of having a Portuguese Massive Open Online Course (MOOC) using the resources in *Bate Papo* will also be considered as the project takes its form. The advantage of using a MOOC is that they provide access to students from all over the world for free.

## 4. Conclusion

When creating new foreign language materials, one should have in mind the ever more diverse audience they are addressing so that a more fruitful, effective, engaging, and real environment is achieved[5]. In addition to the paucity of studies and approaches devoted to the inclusion of marginalised groups in Portuguese language activities, the inclusion of sociological categories such as dialect, sociolect, ethnicity, sexual orientation, and religion, among others, in current textbooks is sometimes not acknowledged or, if so, accounted for in a side note (for a more in-depth discussion on queer pedagogy in Portuguese language materials, see Neto, 2016). This case study is meant to open the dialogue in terms of the representation in the classroom of sociological groups other than the majority and far from the idea of a unified non-real language. Being more accessible, open, real, and free, the new e-textbook is not so much concerned with how to speak proper Portuguese in one way, but how to use Portuguese in different settings and allowing one's individuality.

## Acknowledgements

Thank you Ana Cristina B. Salomão and Nildicéia Rocha from the Universidade Estadual Paulista and Leandro Rodrigues Alves Diniz from the Universidade Federal de Minas Gerais. We are also grateful to the Centre for Latin American

---

5. Otlowski (2003) stresses this same need in the case of English as a Foreign Language (EFL): "the teacher and the textbook are the two most important and immediate cultural links between the student's native culture and the target foreign culture. If the influential roles of the teacher and the textbook are accepted, then the way the textbook portrays the various people in the target society and the way those people are shown to communicate will directly affect EFL students' choices of language when communicating with native speakers. This has important implications for the EFL teacher and for textbook selection" (p. 2).

Studies at the University of Florida and to our institutions, the University of Washington and the University of Pennsylvania. This e-textbook has also been supported through the UW Libraries Open Textbook Award. Last but not least, a massive thank you to Sarah Sweeney, the project coordinator at the Centre for Open Educational Resources and Language Learning (COERLL) at the University of Texas, Austin. Sarah has been a long-term supporter of this project. We cannot forget all the students, language instructors, and volunteers involved in this project as well. Thank you very much! Obrigado!

## References

Hilliard, A. D. (2014). A critical examination of representation and culture in four English language textbooks. *Language Education in Asia, 5*(2), 238-252. https://doi.org/10.5746/leia/14/v5/i2/a06/hilliard

Kubota, R., Austin, T., & Saito-Abbott, Y. (2003). Diversity and inclusion of sociopolitical issues in foreign language classrooms: an exploratory survey. *Foreign Language Annals, 36*(1), 12-24. https://doi.org/10.1111/j.1944-9720.2003.tb01928.x

Looney D., & Lusin, N. (2018). *Enrollments in languages other than english in United States institutions of higher education, Summer 2016 and Fall 2016: preliminary report*. Modern Language Association of America. https://www.mla.org/content/download/83540/2197676/2016-Enrollments-Short-Report.pdf

Mendonça, J. T. de (2012). O ensino de língua portuguesa e a sua relação com a inclusão/exclusão social. *Anais do SIELP, 2*(1), 1-13. http://www.ileel.ufu.br/anaisdosielp/wp-content/uploads/2014/07/volume_2_artigo_151.pdf

Neto, J. N. (2016). Pedagogia Queer e Ensino: a representação LGBT nos livros de português como língua estrangeira. In I. Fortunato, R. S. Guimarães & V. Vergueiro (Eds), *Gênero e Cultura: Perspectivas Formativas* (pp. 23-35). Edições Hipóteses.

Otlowski, M. (2003). Ethnic diversity and gender bias in EFL textbooks. *Asian EFL Journal, 5*, 1-15. http://www.asian-efl-journal.com/june_03_mo.pdf

Pérez-Leroux, A., & Glass, W. R. (2000). Linguistic diversity and inclusion in the foreign language classroom. *Foreign Language Annals, 33*(1), 58-62. https://doi.org/10.1111/j.1944-9720.2000.tb00890.x

# 2. Creating and implementing open educational resources for the Spanish as a Heritage Language classroom

### Evelyn Durán Urrea[1] and Jocelly G. Meiners[2]

## Abstract

The development of language courses designed specifically for Spanish heritage learners has recently gained much attention at all levels of education in the US. Since heritage learners started to acquire the language since childhood at home, their needs are different from those of students in the traditional foreign language classroom. To fulfill these needs, Spanish heritage teachers at all levels are creating programs and materials to serve this student population. The Heritage Spanish web-based community (https://heritagespanish.coerll.utexas.edu), hosted by the Center for Open Educational Resources and Language Learning (COERLL), was created as a space for Spanish teachers to collaborate, share, and communicate about the teaching and learning of Spanish as a heritage language (https://www.coerll.utexas.edu/coerll/about-coerll). A specific example of the design and implementation of Open Educational Resources (OERs) in a Spanish as a heritage language course is found at Lehman College from the City University of New York (CUNY), which serves a significant student population of Hispanic origin.

Keywords: heritage learners, heritage Spanish, open educational resources, web-based community.

---

1. Lehman College, The City University of New York, New York, United States; evelyn.duran@lehman.cuny.edu

2. The University of Texas, Austin, Texas, United States; jocelly@utexas.edu

How to cite this chapter: Durán Urrea, E., & Meiners, J. G. (2019). Creating and implementing open educational resources for the Spanish as a Heritage Language classroom. In A. Comas-Quinn, A. Beaven & B. Sawhill (Eds), *New case studies of openness in and beyond the language classroom* (pp. 23-36). Research-publishing.net. https://doi.org/10.14705/rpnet.2019.37.964

Chapter 2

## 1. Context of the project

The importance of heritage language education has been extensively recognized in the US. In this context, the term *heritage language* applies to languages other than English that are considered minority languages. Instruction of Spanish as a Heritage Language (SHL) in the US has grown considerably in the last decades and the number of students of Hispanic descent enrolling in Spanish courses has generated a need to create programs that suit the specific needs of this population. Heritage speakers have learned the language in their childhood at home but once formal education begins, English becomes dominant. Heritage speakers of Spanish typically acquire total or partial proficiency naturalistically rather than through classroom instruction (i.e. Valdés, 2001).

When heritage speakers study the heritage language that they have some proficiency in or a cultural connection to through family, community, or country of origin, in an academic setting, these students are referred to as Heritage Learners (HLs). HLs are distinct from second language learners and have different needs. Second language learners do not possess previous knowledge of the language to be studied, have no oral proficiency, and have a limited vocabulary and command of grammar structures. By contrast, HLs might possess oral proficiency and native knowledge of the local vocabulary and grammar structures, as well as sociolinguistic, cultural, and pragmatic nuances of the language.

Approaches employed by SHL programs are different from those teaching methods used by Spanish as a Second Language (SSL) programs. In SSL courses, teaching assumes a level of competence of zero amongst students, whereas in SHL courses, teaching must account for a measurable level of competence in the language skills of HLs. Therefore, the SHL teacher must move forward by building upon these existing language skills. Similarly, the interests of HLs cannot be satisfied by SSL courses, which focus on developing elementary vocabulary and oral skills, and where the culture taught carries unconnected materials to the HLs' cultural knowledge.

Considering the needs of HLs, there is a lack of readily available commercial resources despite their growing popularity. Heritage Spanish programs remain underserved by commercial textbook publishers. What this means for teachers who teach HLs is that they are left either to adapt the few published materials that do exist to fit their courses and programs, or else to create their own. For this audience, OERs can provide critical materials tailored to these types of learners.

In the past few years, the use of OERs for language learning has been explored and implemented. Blyth (2014) emphasizes the value of OERs by arguing that

> "open education emphasizes the use of digital materials that are easily edited and personalized, an anytime/anywhere approach to learning, the integration of knowledge and social networks in order to connect people to ideas, and a belief that knowledge is best understood as a creative process of co-constructed meaning within a community of practice" (p. 662).

The positive impact that OERs can have on language teaching has been shown with languages such as English (Altunay, 2013) and French (Blyth, 2012). In this article, we illustrate how OERs can help fill the gap of materials for teaching Spanish as a HL. We first describe COERLL, a repository of OERs created by a community of Heritage Spanish teachers, and then we describe a specific example of OERs being used for a particular population of Spanish HLs at Lehman College, CUNY, where the goal is to apply OERs to promote positive cultural models and develop bilingual literacy skills. By creating and using OERs, teachers at Lehman College seek to support pertinent and current cultural topics that emerge from the students' local communities and to focus on the linguistic and academic needs of the heritage language learners.

## 2. Intended outcomes

As was previously mentioned, there is a growing number of Spanish HLs around the country. At all levels of instruction (K-12 and higher education), teachers are

Chapter 2

faced with the task of creating courses that target this specific learner population. Given the variety of Spanish speaking countries from which immigrants arrive and the many different varieties of Spanish spoken in the US, the populations of HLs are quite different from one part of the country to another. In addition, the access to the heritage language is different for each student population depending on their family situation and their geographic location. For example, HLs residing in Miami, Florida live in a very different sociolinguistic environment than those living in Des Moines, Iowa, in El Paso, Texas, or in New York City, where the Hispanic populations come from different parts of the Spanish speaking world (Cuba, Nicaragua, Venezuela, Mexico, Puerto Rico, etc.). In some of the places where these HLs live, Spanish is heard and used everywhere, whereas in others, HLs only hear Spanish in their homes and with their families.

Given the wide variety of situations faced by SHL student populations around the country, the students' needs for language instruction are different from one school to another. This situation makes it difficult to find language learning materials that teachers can use in their classrooms. As was mentioned earlier, there is a lack of readily available commercial materials for SHL courses, and thus teachers all over the country at all levels of instruction are creating their own materials or adapting existing materials for their own student population's needs. For this reason, the use of OERs is an excellent way to address the situation. Using open source materials, teachers can access resources, modify, and adapt them to their own needs. For example, teachers in Southern California and Southern Florida might use similar materials to teach a particular grammar concept, but they might introduce the concept using relevant readings for each student population, such as the topic of migrant workers in California and the topic of Cuban immigration in Florida.

To support the endeavors of SHL teachers at all levels of instruction around the country, the Heritage Spanish website and community was created to serve as a repository and sharing platform for OERs. One example of a resource that has been shared on the Heritage Spanish website are the open source materials that were compiled and created for a SHL course at Lehman College, CUNY. Using open source material from other institutions and some original materials, we have put together a SHL course that fulfills our students' needs. Given the amount of work it takes to create such a course, it is encouraged for teachers to share their work and help other teachers facing similar needs.

## 3. Nuts and bolts

### 3.1. The Heritage Spanish website and community

Figure 1. Screenshot of the Heritage Spanish website homepage (https://heritagespanish.coerll.utexas.edu)

COERLL is a National Foreign Language Resource Center. There are 16 of these centers around the country, funded by the US Department of Education with the goal of helping the mission of teaching and learning foreign languages. Each of the centers has a different focus. COERLL is hosted by the University of Texas, Austin, and its focus is to promote the creation of OERs for language learning and instruction, and to disseminate these materials over the internet. COERLL supports projects for K-12 and higher education in many languages such as Arabic, German, French, Chinese, Portuguese, and Spanish.

COERLL has several resources available for learning and teaching Spanish; one of them is the Heritage Spanish website and community (see Figure 1 above).

The Heritage Spanish website serves as a space for teachers to collaborate, share, and communicate with other teachers about the teaching and learning of SHL at any level of instruction. The website serves K-12 teachers as well as higher education teachers, and it contains a forum where teachers can sign up to post announcements and questions or start discussions. They can also sign up to receive a periodic newsletter with useful information for the Heritage Spanish community. There is also a section on the website with current affairs, and another section where you can learn about events that are taking place around the country, such as workshops or conferences that are relevant for the Heritage Spanish field.

Most importantly, the website aims to be a repository of OERs for teachers who are searching for materials for their SHL courses. It contains many resources that might be useful for Heritage Spanish teachers, such as research articles, newspaper articles, classroom activities, lesson plans, syllabi, and many others (Figure 2).

Through the Heritage Spanish website and community, COERLL aims to promote the creation of OERs and the subsequent sharing of those OERs. Teachers who create lesson plans, activities, or other resources are encouraged to use a Creative Commons license (https://creativecommons.org) to share their work openly. The Heritage Spanish website licensing page (https://heritagespanish.coerll.utexas.edu/licensing-page/), states the following:

> "Here at the [COERLL], we add Creative Commons licenses on all of the materials that we create for teaching and learning. These licenses

indicate that the content is 'open' and foster the respectful sharing of ideas. We encourage you to use open materials and to add Creative Commons licenses to materials you create, so that users of your work give you proper credit and understand what rights they do or do not have to reuse, modify, redistribute, or sell your content".

Figure 2.  Screenshot of the Heritage Spanish website resources page (https://heritagespanish.coerll.utexas.edu/resources/)

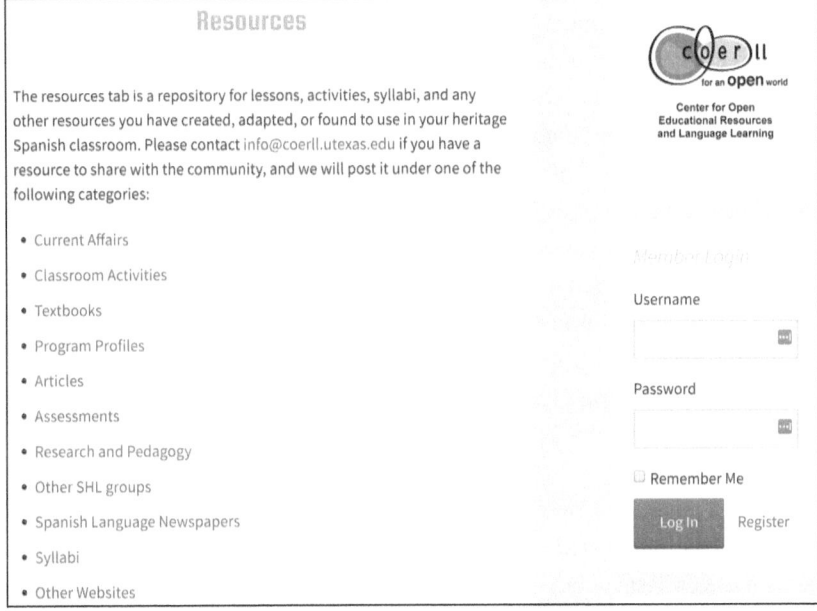

Some of the ways that COERLL promotes the OER movement is by attending relevant conferences and sharing information. Also, several small grants are given each year to selected teachers who propose interesting projects that will produce OER materials to share with the community. In addition, every summer COERLL hosts a workshop about SHL instruction with guest speakers who are experts in the field. Teachers from all levels of education and from all over the country attend the workshop to learn about teaching SHL, and also to learn about the creation and dissemination of OERs. The Heritage Spanish website hosts

Chapter 2

a thriving and growing community of Heritage Spanish teachers from around the country, and it will continue to expand as the need for these OERs for SHL instruction continues to grow.

## 3.2. Using, adapting, and creating OERs for a Heritage Spanish course at Lehman College

As mentioned above, for a long time there has been an absence of available Heritage Spanish commercial textbooks and materials. This absence has left SHL teachers to adapt the limited published materials that do exist for their courses or to create their own, which is time consuming. For this case study, we will focus on a beginner-intermediate SHL course to illustrate the design and implementation of OERs in the classroom. This course is offered at Lehman College, CUNY, located in The Bronx. This institution serves a student population that is 52.5% of Hispanic/Latinx[3] origin. In the design of this course, materials were gathered from many diverse sources that focused on the SHL populations of Dominican and Mexican origin at Lehman College. To be able to provide the volume of necessary and suitable materials, it was imperative to search for, adapt, and create materials for this specific course. It will be clear to any teacher familiar with compiling materials from different books that copyright restrictions present a large problem, and this is why the use of OERs becomes a lifesaver.

These OER materials were formulated for this specific SHL course, designed to fit the topics appropriate to this level in a multi-level curriculum. The goal in using these OER materials was to help the students develop language skills such as reading, listening, speaking, and writing and at the same time, work on their cultural and heritage knowledge. A website using WordPress was created as a reference to find the OER materials for the course (Figure 3).

To illustrate the process for creating and implementing the materials, we will discuss the use of OER materials during the first three weeks of the semester.

---

[3]. We use the term Latinx to demonstrate a gender inclusive stance with those not included in the gendered uses of Latino or Latina.

Figure 3. Screenshot of the OER website for SHL course (https://spa114.commons.gc.cuny.edu/)

> **SPA 114 Spanish for Heritage Speakers 2** *Course Site for SPA 114*
>
> Home  Week 1  Week 2  Week 3  Week 4  Week 5  Week 6  Week 7  Week 8  Week 9  Week 10  Week 11  Week 12  Week 13
>
> **Elementary Spanish Heritage Speakers 2**    Search
>
> *Bienvenidos a la clase.* This is a beginning course with emphasis on elements of grammatical structures and practice in reading, writing and oral exposition. Spanish 114 is the second level of a course designed for bilingual or Spanish heritage students to allow these students to obtain and develop the necessary skills to communicate in standard or academic Spanish. Spanish 114 is designed for students who have been reared in a Spanish-speaking environment and speak or understand some Spanish as a result of having heard it in the home and community by parents or grandparents, family, friends, and neighbors.

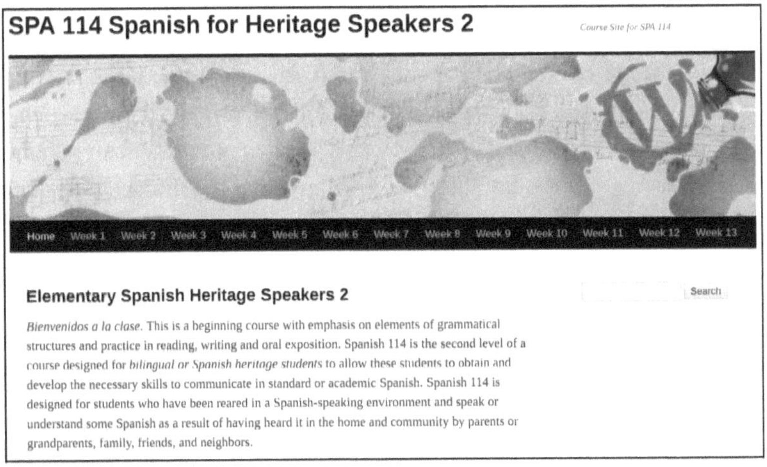

*3.2.1. Materials in Week 1: literacy Skills*

In the first week of class, the following OER materials focused on transferring reading skills from English to Spanish. Since English becomes the language of instruction for heritage speakers of Spanish once they enter the US school system, they tend to acquire stronger literacy skills in English than in Spanish. An effective strategy to develop proficiency in Spanish is to transfer skills that the learner already possesses from the dominant language. The following activity applies this type of transfer:

> *Activity 1*: *Transference of reading skills*. The first activity developed by the teacher was an exercise on reading in Spanish using skills students already have a good command of in English, such as finding the meaning of a word through the context in the reading. A video with specific instructions on how to work on the activity was created for this exercise (https://spa114.commons.gc.cuny.edu/week-1/). It allowed learners to work actively on reading skills that they usually do not apply when reading in Spanish. To maximize classroom learning and integration

time, the activity was assigned as homework and on the following class section students discussed their findings.

*Activity 2: Maintenance and loss of Spanish.* In the same week, the teacher selected an OER podcast to discuss the importance of learning and maintaining Spanish and to talk and reflect about students' personal connections to Spanish. The teacher created a questionnaire about the podcast to guide the discussion about the topic. Students listened to the podcast at home followed by a discussion in class guided by the questionnaire provided in Week 1 materials (Figure 4).

Figure 4. Questionnaire to discuss podcast (https://www.pri.org/stories/2016-0128/ok-dad-why-did-you-kill-spanish-our-family)

---

Escucha el podcast y contesta las siguientes preguntas. **Para entregar.**

Nombre: _____

1. ¿Qué lenguas habla tu madre o padre? ¿Cuál lengua habla o hablan más fluidamente?

2. ¿Cuál fue la primera vez que al papá de Bradley le llamaron "beaner" (*frijolero*)? ¿Qué crees que significa esa palabra?

3. ¿Por qué el papá de Bradley no siente que habla español con fluidez?

4. ¿Qué dice Bradley a su abuelita en el teléfono?

5. ¿Por qué crees que el español dejó de hablarse en la casa de Bradley?

6. ¿Crees que el papá de Bradley mató el español en su casa? ¿Por qué?

Evelyn Durán Urrea

---

### 3.2.2. Materials in Week 2: cultural heritage

In the second week of the semester, materials selected and created focused on learning and discussing the Latinx population and the history of Spanish in the US and to connect these topics to the students' own heritage. The example material selected is an OER reading with questions created by the teacher to guide the discussion about the reading (https://spa114.commons.gc.cuny.edu/week-2/).

*3.2.3. Exercises in Week 3: grammar*

In Week 3, the OER materials were related to grammar topics and were adopted from the repositories in the COERLL Heritage Spanish website. Grammar instruction for SHLs differs from traditional instruction for second language learners. HLs benefit from instruction which focuses on form and understanding of how grammar works from a descriptive perspective (Burgo, 2015). Grammar materials should be authentic and show different Spanish varieties. In this manner, the grammar materials used in the course come from the COERLL Heritage Spanish website, as it is one of the only OER repositories that focuses on a descriptive perspective for SHL (Figure 5).

Figure 5. Screenshot of an OER grammar repository from the COERLL Heritage Spanish website (http://grammar.spanishintexas.org/verbs/future/)

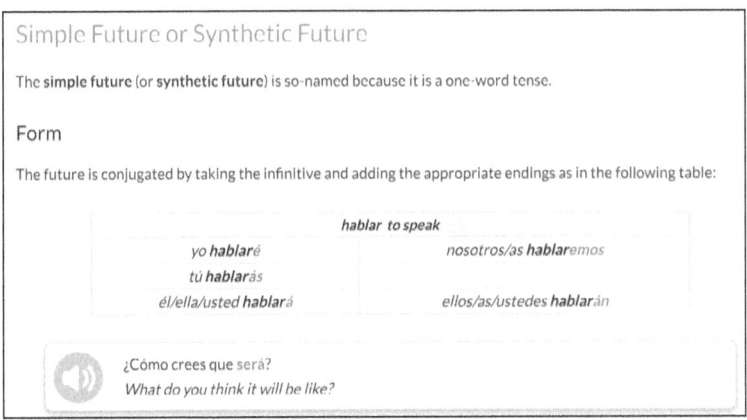

The 13 week OER materials website designed for a SHL course at this level, has materials for each week of the semester implemented with the course curriculum. The variety of topics all work towards the same two goals of the class: (1) to develop the HLs' language skills while allowing them to apply those skills in academic and professional settings and (2) to work on the HLs' knowledge about their own cultural and linguistic heritage.

### 3.2.4. Evaluation of OER materials

The use of OERs in this course has made it possible to use materials in a transformative way and to create critical awareness for students. The benefits that OERs provided in teaching this course were varied. The teacher had the choice to adapt and customize lesson plans according to the course needs and the students' interests. Also, creating and curating these materials allowed the use of content that was tailored specifically to the students' cultural backgrounds or their particular interests, incorporating actual topics or local language and culture that traditional textbooks do not address.

Students and teachers were able to print, reproduce, and modify the course materials without being confined by copyright restrictions. Moreover, the use of OERs was beneficial to the students from an economic perspective. OERs can be a response on how to balance costs in public education since they can offer considerable savings as an alternative to buying expensive textbooks. Students in this course extensively expressed their appreciation for the reduced economic burden of not having to buy a textbook. They also voiced that OERs allowed them to follow the course easily and gave them flexibility to access the materials from anywhere. Furthermore, students commented that these types of materials kept the course interesting and improved their motivation for learning. They also felt that without a textbook their learning style was more hands on, and they considered OERs one of the best components of the class. Overall, the use of OERs was a great asset in creating a course to serve our students in the teaching of SHL.

## 4. Conclusions

During the past few years, the Heritage Spanish website and community has served many SHL teachers at different levels of education who have searched for resources to use in their classrooms. It has also helped in many ways as support for SHL teacher training endeavors and as support to teachers who have been tasked with creating a Heritage Spanish program in their institution.

This has all been possible through the creation and dissemination of open educational materials. A great example can be found at Lehman College, where open source materials have been extremely useful, as they have been used to create and adapt course materials that are specifically tailored to the needs of their HL population, focusing on promoting positive cultural models and developing language skills.

As the HL population grows throughout the country, it is our hope that with the support of the Heritage Spanish website and community, more institutions will follow their lead. In addition, we hope to inspire SHL teachers in K-12 and higher education institutions to create, use, and adapt more open source materials so that they can best serve the particular needs of their HL student populations and to use these materials in a transformative way to create critical awareness for students.

## Acknowledgements

We are grateful to the COERLL team (Carl Blyth, Sarah Sweeney, Nathalie Steinfeld Childre) for their hard work and support with the Heritage Spanish project.

We would like to acknowledge Stacy Katz and the CUNY OER Scale-up Initiative from Lehman College Leonard Lief Library for their support.

## References

Altunay, D. (2013). The role of open educational resources in english language learning and teaching. *Computer-Assisted Language Learning and Teaching, 3*(2), 97-107. https://doi.org/10.4018/ijcallt.2013040106

Blyth, C. (2012). Opening up foreign language education with open educational resources: the case of *Français interactif*. In F. Rubio & J. Thoms (Eds), *Hybrid language teaching and learning: exploring theoretical, pedagogical and curricular issues* (pp. 196-218). Heinle.

Blyth, C. (2014). Open educational resources and the new classroom ecology. *The Modern Language Journal, 98*(2), 662-664. https://doi.org/10.1111/modl.12096

Burgo, C. (2015). Grammar teaching approaches for heritage learners of Spanish. In A. J. Moeller (Ed.), *Learn languages, explore cultures, transform lives* (pp. 217-233). Selected Papers from the 2015 Central States Conference on the Teaching of Foreign Languages.

Valdés, G. (2001). Heritage language students: profiles and possibilities. In J. K. Peyton, D. Ranard & S. McGinnis (Eds), *Heritage languages in America: preserving a national resource* (pp. 37-77). Center for Applied Linguistics.

ically used for
# 3 Italian Open Education: virtual reality immersions for the language classroom

### Margherita Berti[1]

## Abstract

This case study describes the development of a free-to-use online platform for storing, sharing, and accessing 360-degree Virtual Reality (VR) videos. Although in the past VR was mostly used for gaming purposes, in recent years it has become increasingly popular in numerous areas, including education. In the field of language learning, little is still known about the development and use of open VR materials as well as their affordances and constraints. The current project addresses this gap by illustrating the practical steps taken to develop an open education platform, by investigating undergraduate students' attitudes toward the implementation of VR in the language classroom, and by discussing pedagogical insights about how openly licensed VR resources can be used to foster students' learning. Overall, this case study revealed that VR Open Educational Resources (OERs) can be powerful vehicles to promote inclusion, innovation, and engagement.

Keywords: virtual reality, open educational resources, Italian, CALL.

## 1. Context of the project

In recent years numerous technologies have emerged in the field of language learning and pedagogy and educators are integrating technology tools in

---

1. The University of Arizona, Tucson, Arizona, United States; berti@email.arizona.edu; https://orcid.org/0000-0002-6572-921X

**How to cite this chapter:** Berti, M. (2019). Italian Open Education: virtual reality immersions for the language classroom. In A. Comas-Quinn, A. Beaven & B. Sawhill (Eds), *New case studies of openness in and beyond the language classroom* (pp. 37-47). Research-publishing.net. https://doi.org/10.14705/rpnet.2019.37.965

# Chapter 3

the classroom setting to supplement the traditional textbook and to enhance students' learning (Blake, 2013). Among the latest technologies there is VR, a computer-generated experience that simulates physical presence in real or imagined environments (Van Kerrebroeck, Brengman, & Willems, 2017). While research studies concerning VR in the fields of medicine, history, and architecture abound (e.g. Abdullah, Kassim, & Sanusi, 2017; Fabola, Miller, & Fawcett, 2015; Morandi & Tremari, 2017; Talbot, 2018), in the area of language education only a few studies have looked at the affordances and constraints of immersive VR environments. Lin and Lan (2015) investigated VR research trends in four top Computer Assisted Language Learning (CALL) journals from 2004 to 2013. Results showed that out of 811 published articles, only 29 empirical studies concerned VR. Furthermore, to date there appear to be no studies exploring the creation and use of VR OERs for language education. This dearth of studies prompted this author, a doctoral student in Second Language Acquisition and Teaching and Italian instructor at the University of Arizona, to develop a platform named Italian Open Education (https://italianopeneducation.com/), an independent project which offers a collection of openly licensed and open access 360-degree VR videos. This new tool was conceived to help Italian language learners better understand, at no expense, the many facets of the target culture which is frequently presented in a static manner and as factual information in traditional language textbooks (McConachy & Hata, 2013).

## 2. Intended outcomes

The main purpose of Italian Open Education was to support and enhance language learning using innovative resources which would not financially burden students. The platform was specifically developed for Italian students, whether enrolled in language courses or studying Italian on their own. Six specific outcomes were set:

- to produce new 360-degree VR materials tailored to the study of the Italian language and culture;

- to provide language teachers with openly licensed innovative pedagogical resources which promote cultural awareness;

- to provide language students from different backgrounds and socioeconomic statuses the opportunity to be included and participate in conversations regarding the target culture;

- to understand students' attitudes and beliefs toward the use of open VR resources in the educational setting;

- to increase students' engagement; and

- to provide individuals all over the world the opportunity to explore the Italian culture at no cost.

In order to achieve these goals, the author recorded 360-degree VR videos in Italy, uploaded them on YouTube, marked them with a Creative Commons (CC) Attribution-NonCommercial-ShareAlike 3.0 License (CC BY-NC-SA 3.0), and shared them on the online platform. Other videos recorded by YouTube users, which either have the above-mentioned CC License or a Standard YouTube License, were gathered and shared on Italian Open Education. After the platform was launched in September 2018, students enrolled in beginner and intermediate Italian courses used such resources to explore Italian settings in their multiple facets and participated in teacher-led discussions to foster cultural awareness. Data from students was collected to further understand how VR OERs might be integrated in the language classroom.

## 3. Nuts and bolts

VR has the potential to transform language education since it offers users the opportunity to be immersed in authentic experiences otherwise inaccessible due to geographical constraints. Nowadays, most students are not able to study abroad and authentically explore the target country. VR OERs, which can be

Chapter 3

reused and adapted according to teachers and students' needs, promote inclusion by allowing students to be virtually immersed and physically present in non-physical yet culturally authentic environments (Blyth, 2018) and further develop their awareness of the target culture. Several steps were followed to develop, launch, and use Italian Open Education.

## 3.1. Recording and creating 360-degree VR videos

In order to create 360-degree VR videos, special equipment was purchased by the author. The Xiaomi Mijia Mi Dual-Lens Sphere 360 Camera was the chosen tool to be used in Italy to record authentic environments. This camera features a 360-degree field of view which captures an entire environment, in any direction, as opposed to conventional digital cameras which produce videos by focusing on one fixed angle.

In December 2017, this author flew to Italy and recorded many videos using the 360 camera in her hometown Bergamo, as well as Milan. The choice of locations to record was dictated by the desire to show students everyday Italian environments (e.g. a plaza, a coffee shop, a restaurant, a mall, a street, etc.) as well as some environments that are commonly represented in Italian textbooks (e.g. Galleria Vittorio Emanuele II in Milan). The camera was placed in strategic locations within the environments and it was remotely controlled through a smartphone. Videos were recorded for about 3 minutes so that when viewed by students the various Italian settings would appear lively and in movement, as opposed to a static image or a very short video. A total of 14 videos were recorded.

The videos were transferred to a laptop and processed with the Spatial Media Metadata Injector software (https://github.com/google/spatial-media/releases/tag/v2.1), an open-access YouTube software which adds metadata to a video indicating that the file contains a 360-degree video. The videos were uploaded to a dedicated YouTube channel named 'Italian Open Education'. To facilitate web searches, videos were named 'IOE' (the acronym of the platform) along with the Italian word of a specific environment, for instance 'piazza' or 'ristorante'. Videos on YouTube were shared under the education category and marked with a CC BY-NC-SA 3.0, which allows users to adapt the resources for non-commercial purposes and share them with the same license, while still giving appropriate credit to the author. Figure 1 shows the Italian Open Education YouTube channel (https://www.youtube.com/channel/UCdElEVQ9PRJ6yRQ41_NHmuA).

Figure 1.  The Italian Open Education YouTube channel

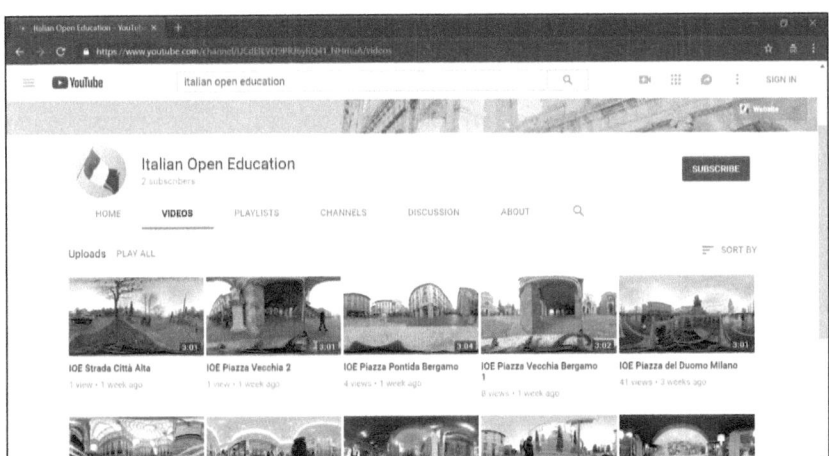

### 3.2.   Creating the Italian Open Education platform

The Italian Open Education platform was developed by the author on WordPress (https://wordpress.org/), a free and open-source content management system based on PHP and MySQL. WordPress was chosen for this project for its simple interface and the numerous plugins and templates available which reduce development costs and deployment time. The platform focused on collecting 360-degree VR videos that represent Italian environments as well as instructions on how to create, access, and view the videos. First, the 14 videos previously recorded in Italy were organized in different categories and embedded in the platform. Following, additional 360-degree VR videos representing Italy were searched on YouTube. Although most of the found videos had a Standard YouTube License, some videos presented a CC License signifying that individuals are sharing innovative digital content with the desire of making such resources accessible and adaptable to others. The newly found videos were also categorized and embedded in the platform. Each video was briefly described in Italian along with the type of license which characterized them, and the authors of the videos were credited.

Since VR is still an emerging technology in the field of language learning and pedagogy, two specific web-pages addressing how to use the videos and the equipment needed to view the resources were created. A 'How to' (https://italianopeneducation.com/how-to/) web-page was created to provide a step-by-step explanation of how to view the content in VR. The web-page explains that users need to download the YouTube app on their smartphone, open any 360-degree video in the app (using the keyword '360' before the name of the environment facilitates finding 360-degree videos; e.g. 360 street), and click on the small headset icon on the bottom right of the video. The smartphone screen will then divide in two, giving users a sense of depth once the device is inserted in a headset such as Google Cardboard (https://vr.google.com/cardboard/). Although there are many VR headsets on the market, Google Cardboard is among the most economical ones and when utilized with a smartphone and specific applications (e.g. YouTube) it creates a stereoscopic effect, which adds an illusion of depth to a flat image and gives users the illusion of presence in virtual environments.

Last, the 'Equipment' (https://italianopeneducation.com/equipment/) web-page on the platform addresses the tools that are needed to experience VR environments as well as the specific equipment that was used by the author to create VR resources. To view the 360-degree videos in VR, users need a smartphone, the YouTube app, a simple viewer such as Google Cardboard, and optional headphones to create an even more immersive experience.

### 3.3. Students' attitudes and beliefs

VR supports language educators by giving them the opportunity to engage students in experiential learning, that is, the process of learning by doing (Kolb,

1984). Students are immersed in 360-degree authentic virtual environments and can move their head in any direction and choose where to focus their attention, thus creating personalized learning experiences. Rather than telling students what to think about the foreign culture, with VR, students are given the tools and materials to compare, contrast, and discover cultural insights. The opportunity to experience the target culture by being highly immersed in authentic virtual environments is without precedent. This open platform promotes inclusion since it provides equal access to authentic virtual experiences and it is especially beneficial to those students who are not able to study abroad since it supports cultural learning in immersive environments of the target country.

Considering the paucity of studies investigating the use of VR for language learning, this project also aimed at exploring undergraduate students' beliefs and attitudes toward the use of 360-degree VR videos in the classroom setting. During a grant-funded, student/faculty interaction out-of-class event, 14 students enrolled in beginner and intermediate Italian courses were given a Google Cardboard headset each and were instructed on how to use such a device.

Prior to viewing four immersive 360-degree VR Italian environments, participants completed a survey designed to assess their experiences with technology for language learning as well as their interest and knowledge of the target culture. Participants stated having not used VR in the language classroom or for other educational purposes. All 14 (100%) students reported that technology enhances language learning and that when used in the classroom it is enjoyable and fun. All participants also reported that studying the Italian culture is important to them, however, only 32% felt familiar with the target culture.

Next, participants explored four 360-degree VR videos with the use of their smartphones, Google Cardboard, and headphones. Prior to each video, participants were told about the environment they were going to see (i.e. a street in Florence, an opera theater in Modena, a bakery in Bergamo, and a plaza in Milan) and they were asked to write a pre-reflection about colors, sounds, materials, and people that they expected to see. The pre-reflections helped students explore their understanding and perhaps their stereotyping of Italian environments before the viewings occurred. After each viewing, participants wrote post-reflections, explained whether what they saw was similar or different from what they previously expected, and expanded on their own virtual experience.

Students then participated in teacher-led conversations addressing the cultural aspects of the experienced environments. Discussions and written reflections revealed that by using VR OERs, participants noticed unique cultural layers that they might not notice in traditional pedagogical resources. For instance, students were surprised by the dimensions of buildings and how narrow streets were. The height and width of an environment particularly stands out in VR since everything appears in real-life dimensions, an impressive feature that traditional 'flat' videos do not have. When students were told that they would be virtually standing in an Italian bakery they wrote that they expected to see pastries, desserts, and a baker with a white hat. However, in Italy, most bakeries (in Italian 'panetteria') sell bread and savory foods, such as pizza by the slice, thus the viewing took students by surprise. Students also expected to see artifacts 'everywhere' while exploring the street in Florence. Instead, students were surprised by the modest street without as much art as they anticipated. These particular cultural aspects, usually noticed when travelling abroad to a foreign country, are freely available today to language students in the classroom through VR OERs.

Lastly, participants completed a post-survey where they expressed attitudes and concerns about the potential use of VR materials in the educational setting. All participants stated that the virtual experiences were useful to understanding more about Italy, 65% were interested in using VR in the classroom context, and 84% reported that the experience increased their motivation and engagement. A participant stated that such virtual experiences brought her Italian instructor's cultural explanations to life, while another participant reported that, unlike regular classroom lectures where everything is filtered through a teacher's point of view, VR gives individuals the opportunity to focus on whichever detail catches their attention. This experience created involvement and participants felt as if VR provided them with a more accurate depiction of Italy than the traditional textbook.

Participants also discussed potential drawbacks of using VR technologies in language education. Some students felt dizzy after the third viewing, while others were concerned with the possibility of VR becoming a distracting technology which might take away from learning. This interesting observation is certainly important since, as educators, we need to carefully examine how technology tools can enhance students' learning as well as pedagogical content before fully implementing new technologies in language courses.

## 4. Conclusion

Researchers in the field of CALL have started to investigate theoretically grounded principles to comprehend the pedagogical value of highly immersive virtual reality for language learning purposes (Lin & Lan, 2015), nonetheless this area remains largely unexplored. Today's ubiquitous technologies allow educators to become creators of innovative pedagogical content. In an effort to promote the Italian culture and to create previously inaccessible experiences for language learners, the author developed Italian Open Education, a one-of-a-kind platform that offers VR OERs for students and teachers across the world. The platform was launched in September 2018 and in less than two months it received 552 page views and 77 visitors from various countries such as the United States, Switzerland, Canada, Italy, China, Australia, Belgium, and many more. The VR OERs were tested with language students who were able to 'travel' to Italy, experience, and explore the target culture from the classroom setting. The digital materials marked with a CC License found on Italian Open Education can be reused and adapted, provided that they are shared with the same license and the original source is acknowledged. By sharing open resources, innovation and inclusion can be fostered while supporting students' learning and engagement. This project did not address in what ways highly-immersive VR videos enhance learning more or differently than regular videos, thus further research is needed to explore the similarities and differences between the two. Additionally, the 360-degree VR videos used in this project allowed users to focus their attention on what they preferred, but such videos do not allow for interactions (e.g. entering in specific places, touching objects within the environment, speaking to people, etc.). Further research is needed to shed more light on practical applications, affordances, and constraints of VR OERs in language education.

## Acknowledgements

The author would like to express gratitude to Stefano Maranzana and Jacob Monzingo for their involvement in the research concerning the use of VR in language education. The generous contribution of the Student/Faculty Interaction Grants Program at the University of Arizona is also worth noting.

## References

Abdullah, F., Kassim, M. H. B., & Sanusi, A. N. Z. (2017). Go virtual: exploring augmented reality application in representation of steel architectural construction for the enhancement of architecture education. *Advanced Science Letters, 23*(2), 804-808. https://doi.org/10.1166/asl.2017.7449

Blake, R. J. (2013). *Brave new digital classroom: technology and foreign language learning*. Georgetown University Press.

Blyth, C. (2018). Immersive technologies and language learning. *Foreign Language Annals, 51*(1), 225-232. https://doi.org/10.1111/flan.12327

Fabola, A., Miller, A., & Fawcett, R. (2015). Exploring the past with Google Cardboard. *Digital Heritage, 1*, 277-284. https://doi.org/10.1109/DigitalHeritage.2015.7413882

Kolb, D. A. (1984). *Experiential learning: experience as the source of learning and development* (Vol. 1). Prentice-Hall.

Lin, T. J., & Lan, Y. J. (2015). Language learning in virtual reality environments: past, present, and future. *Journal of Educational Technology & Society, 18*(4), 486-497.

McConachy, T., & Hata, K. (2013). Addressing textbook representations of pragmatics and culture. *ELT journal, 67*(3), 294-301. https://doi.org/10.1093/elt/cct017

Morandi, S., & Tremari, M. (2017). Interactive past: from 3D reconstruction to augmented and virtual reality applied to archaeological heritage. The medieval site of Bastia St. Michele (Cavaion Veronese, Verona, Italy). In *Virtual System & Multimedia (VSMM), 2017 23rd International Conference*. https://doi.org/10.1109/VSMM.2017.8346278

Talbot, T. B. (2018). Making lifelike medical games in the age of virtual reality: an update on "playing games with biology". In *Information Resources Management Association, Virtual and Augmented Reality: Concepts, Methodologies, Tools, and Applications* (pp. 1234-1251). IGI Global. https://doi.org/10.4018/978-1-5225-5469-1.ch059

Van Kerrebroeck, H., Brengman, M., & Willems, K. (2017). Escaping the crowd: an experimental study on the impact of a virtual reality experience in a shopping mall. *Computers in Human Behavior*, 77, 437-450. https://doi.org/10.1016/j.chb.2017.07.019

# 4. Embedding OERs for the development of information literacy in the foreign language classroom

## Odette Gabaudan[1] and Susanna Nocchi[2]

### Abstract

Despite a rapid growth of Open Educational Resource (OER) availability, Thoms and Thoms (2014) note that few empirical studies examine the impact of OERs on foreign language learning and teaching. This paper presents an action research study investigating the embedding of selected components of DigiLanguages, an OER for Digital Literacies (DLs) for Foreign Languages (FL) within a Bachelor of Arts (BA) in International Business and Languages at the Technological University Dublin. Digilanguages.ie is an open portal developed collaboratively by six tertiary education institutions in Ireland. Digital literacies for FL learning and teaching is a key strand in this resource. The study involved two groups of students, one majoring in French and one in Italian. One of the aims of the study was to pilot the portal and identify affordances and constraints of introducing and adapting this OER to the individual FL classroom. Of equal importance was to analyse the potential of the OER to introduce and/or change pedagogical practices in an area that remains largely under investigated, namely DLs for foreign language learning. The study informs future steps in how to use a particular OER to embed units of DLs into FL courses. It also provides insights on developing a new set of professional practices among language teachers.

1. Technological University Dublin, Dublin, Ireland; odette.gabaudan@dit.ie; https://orcid.org/0000-0003-4926-8959

2. Technological University Dublin, Dublin, Ireland; susanna.nocchi@dit.ie; https://orcid.org/0000-0003-1389-8035

**How to cite this chapter:** Gabaudan, O., & Nocchi, S. (2019). Embedding OERs for the development of information literacy in the foreign language classroom. In A. Comas-Quinn, A. Beaven & B. Sawhill (Eds), *New case studies of openness in and beyond the language classroom* (pp. 49-63). Research-publishing.net. https://doi.org/10.14705/rpnet.2019.37.966

Chapter 4

**Keywords: OER, OEP, digital literacies, foreign language learning, French as FL, Italian as FL.**

## 1. Context of the project

Digital technologies in the classroom have long been advocated as an important tool for education both at European (European Commission, 2013) and national level (Irish Department of Education and Skills, 2015, p. 5; National Forum, 2015, p. iii). The diffusion of technologies and their associated DLs is leading us to develop new pedagogies aimed at supporting learners acquiring what is now considered an essential component of life skills (Karpati, 2011).

As DLs are socially, historically, and culturally situated practices, digital fluency is also a core element of FL teaching and learning. With this in mind, the authors designed an action research study aimed to assess the embedding of FL activities for the development of DLs in the FL classroom. The study is anchored in Dudeney, Hockly, and Pegrum's (2014) framework of DLs where DLs are defined as "the individual and social skills needed to effectively interpret, manage, share and create meaning in the growing range of digital communication channels" (p. 2).

The Dudeney et al. (2014) framework comprises different DLs, grouped into four main foci: language, information, connections, and redesign. This study is designed around the information focus, which comprises four literacies: tagging, search, information, and filtering. The FL activities were drawn from DigiLanguages, a multilingual portal offering flexible online support for FL teachers and learners in three broad areas, one being DLs for language development.

The study took place at one of the institutions involved in the DigiLanguages project, Technological University Dublin, where the authors lecture, respectively, in French and in Italian.

## 2. Intended outcomes

As members of the team that developed the portal, the authors' interests were twofold and focussed on the OER both as a tool for teaching and learning and as a trigger to change teachers' educational practices. The authors recognised in their context issues similar to those highlighted by other researchers in the field (Masterman & Wild, 2011; Seaman & Seaman, 2017), namely that the level of awareness and the overall adoption of OERs for FL teaching and learning among colleagues was still rather low. Also, it was noted that OER adoption did not always transfer to Open Educational Practice (OEP). Therefore, this paper focusses on the two teachers' uses of the OER in terms of professional development and its potential to change OEP by highlighting the portal's affordances and constraints in view of its future introduction to the institution's FL courses and in colleagues' OEPs.

## 3. Nuts and bolts

This action research study took place during the 2017/2018 academic year and was conducted using foreign language activities offered on the online portal DigiLanguages.

### 3.1. The DigiLanguages project

The DigiLanguages portal was the result of a national project funded by the Irish National Forum for the Enhancement of Teaching and Learning in Higher Education. The project was carried out by representatives of six Irish higher education institutions and was completed in August 2017. The DigiLanguages portal offers online resources in six languages (English, French, German, Irish, Italian, and Spanish) and activities in three broad areas:

- DL for FL development;

- language learning strategies and practices; and

Chapter 4

- transitions to third level language learning environments.

Each area offers materials with activities for students, activities for teachers with their students, and activities for teachers' Continuous Professional Development (CPD).

The study focussed on DLs for FL development, organised in the DigiLanguages portal following Dudeney et al.'s (2014, p. 6) DLs framework. The subsets of DLs can be seen below (dots on the blue lines, Figure 1).

Figure 1. DigiLanguages portal map

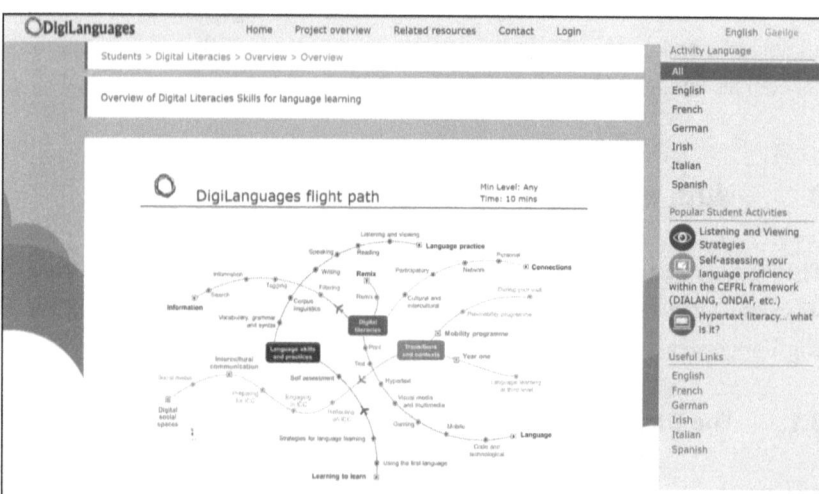

DigiLanguages is freely available and scalable for use. Its contents and activities afford integration into many higher education FL programmes and all materials available on the site use a Creative Commons licence.

## 3.2. Methodology

The research study was designed to test and evaluate the integration of tasks drawn from the portal by one teacher of Italian as an FL and one teacher of

French as an FL within their respective groups of undergraduate students of Business with Italian or with French. The students' language proficiencies varied between levels B1+ and B2+ on the Common European Framework of Reference for languages (CEFR, 2001) and the language tasks were carried out as part of the students' final year course in current affairs. This course aims to develop students' understanding and critical appraisal of current affairs in the countries of their chosen foreign language. While technologically-mediated information literacy is not an explicit learning outcome of the course, it is clearly of particular relevance in a current affairs course.

The following subsections offer an outline of the teachers' approaches by presenting one of the tasks on the portal.

### 3.2.1. Course set up

Each task on the portal is introduced and fully developed in English. It usually contains hyperlinks to videos and websites and generally provides access to additional material. Each language task is also localised for the five other languages.

Both teachers used all available Teacher CPD materials to familiarise themselves with the topic before drawing on relevant DigiLanguages activities for teachers to use with their students. The activities informed the teachers' own lesson plans but in a number of cases these had to be supplemented by further material.

The French teacher worked with her group of seven students for a total of eight hours, and the Italian teacher worked for six hours with a group of six students. The two teachers decided to dedicate three weeks to the theme, with two to three teaching hours per week. Each lesson hour was supplemented by one or two hours of independent learning.

As one of the aims of the research was to explore how individual teachers use and take ownership of an OER, it was decided not to agree on a specific pedagogical approach, nor to agree on a selection of tasks on offer on the portal. Both teachers

Chapter 4

shared their experiences only at the end of the three weeks so as not to influence each other. With a view to help the reader visualise the pedagogical design of the portal, the following section offers an example of one of the language tasks chosen by the two teachers for use in their FL class.

### 3.2.2. The search literacy task

The search literacy task (see Figure 2) is designed to make students aware of how search engines work and how different search engines can filter and offer different results to different individuals. Often FL students do not use country-specific search engines or, if they do, they are not always aware of the cultural, social, political, and/or linguistic nuances differentiating the results that they find. See below the task description in English, as it appears on the teacher tab on DigiLanguages.

Figure 2. Let's search! Search literacy task

**Let's search!**

Min Level: A2
Time: 45 mins

This activity aims to raise students' awareness of how search engines filter results for individuals, and how this can impact on one's studies/work. Before attempting this activity, you may want to point students to the Search literacy... what is it? page or use some of the language specific content to consolidate their vocabulary and written and aural comprehension skills.

**Learning outcomes**

On completion of this activity, students will be able to

- Understand the limitations and personal filtering of search engines
- Narrow down and refine search results

**Technology requirements**

- Internet-enabled computer connected to a data projector
- Internet-enabled student computers or mobile devices (one per student or student pair)
- Search engines (Google, Bing, Yahoo, etc.).
- Microsoft Snipping Tool or any other screenshot capturing tool

**Procedure**

Before the class

1. Before the class, select a search term (word or phrase) that relates to the topic you are working on with your students;
2. Conduct several searches using the same search term
    1. A few minutes apart;
    2. On different devices;
    3. Using different search engines (e.g., Google, Bing, Yahoo, etc.) or regional versions of the same search engine (e.g. Google France/Canada/Belgique, etc., Google Deutschland/Austria/Switzerland, etc.).
3. Make screenshots of the first page of results each time and save them.
4. Prepare a handout or PowerPoint presentation to show in class.
5. Prepare a Google Form for students to fill in in class (Step 2 below), with 3 text boxes for entering search terms (optional).

> In class
> 1. Introduce the subject of the search (for example: finding student accommodation in their target country).
> 2. Ask students to write down 3 search terms, in their target language, relating to the selected topic. This can be done on a piece of paper or by filling in the Google form that you have prepared in advance of the class. Students can work individually or in pairs.
> 3. Read or display the results to the class and discuss the following questions:
>    1. What do the chosen search terms tell you about the authors?
>    2. What kind of information are they looking for?
>    3. What types of results can one expect to get?
> 4. Agree with the whole class on one search term in the target language (for example 'student accommodation').
> 5. Ask students to open their regular search engine and to search for the term agreed in Step 4.
> 6. Ask students to capture a screenshot of their results using Windows Snipping Tool or any other screen capture tool.
> 7. Ask students to repeat Steps 5 and 6 with different search engines (for example Google UK, Google Ireland).
> 8. Ask students to compare and discuss the results of their search (Step 7).
> 9. Ask students to do the same search using the following symbols: +, -, "..." (e.g., +student +accommodation, +student accommodation, -student accommodation, "student accommodation").
> 10. Ask students to compare and discuss the different results.
>
> After class
> Ask students to conduct the same search at home or a new one using a term or terms agreed upon by the class. Students could bring a printout or a screenshot of the first page of search results to class the next day. Let them share their results and compare. What might they say about each student? You may want to point them to Eli Pariser's Ted's talk: Beware online "filter bubbles":

Each group of students worked on the Italian or French version of the Let's search! task, which each teacher adapted for two main reasons. Firstly, the task outlined in the portal requires student access to a computer. Students in both French and Italian had no access to computer labs. As a result, teachers asked them to work on their personal mobile devices and on paper. Secondly, the task described in the portal is very detailed thereby providing users with alternative options that can be adapted to different contexts. Each teacher prepared her own document with all necessary lesson materials for her class. An outline of how each teacher took ownership of the various activities is provided in the next section.

### 3.2.3. The Let's search! task – French

Figure 3.   Localisation of Let's search! for French

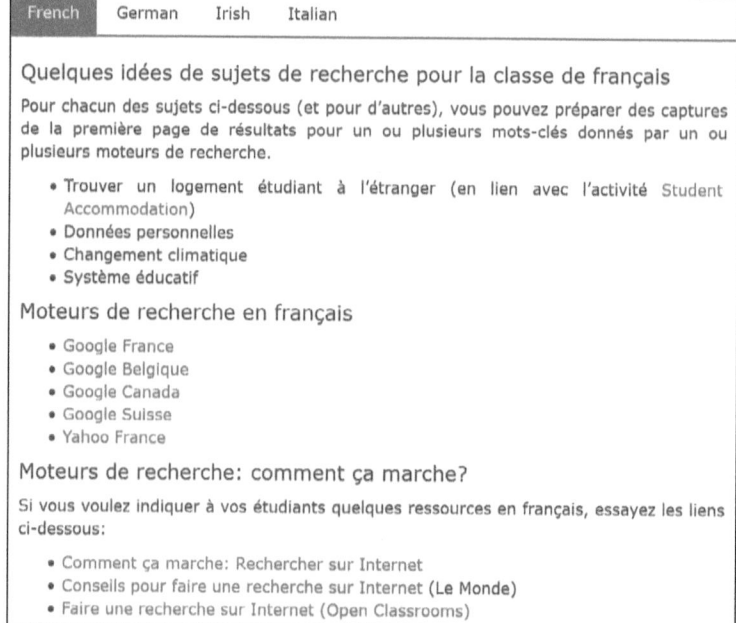

As students were not familiar with Boolean operators and did not appear to use a systematic approach to carrying out searches, the French teacher adapted the Let's search! task (see Figure 3 above) as follows:

- added a pre-discussion task on the students' general approach to carrying out a search and assessing reliable sources of information;

- added a reading activity to familiarise students with concepts and terminology;

- before class, the teacher completed a grid with a number of searches relating to the filter bubble and fake news using different Boolean operators, different browsers, and different country-specific search engines. During class, students were asked to compare and contrast search results before carrying out their own search; and

- after class, students were asked to write a short essay on the topic.

*3.2.4. The Let's search! task – Italian*

Figure 4. Localisation of Let's search! for Italian

Chapter 4

The students of Italian spent two hours on the Let's search! task. The Italian teacher found the guidelines for task preparation and the task outline useful. However, she decided not to follow them in detail, in order to fully adapt the task to suit her group's needs and interests (see Figure 4 above). This was done by adding:

- a general warm-up discussion with students on their experience with search engines;

- pair-work on the 'filter bubble', followed by group discussion;

- a focus on different lexical items in Italian;

- more up-to-date material; and

- a post-task activity requesting students to read links sent to them and prepare for a discussion for the following week on the 'filter bubble' and the impact of algorithms on our life.

## 3.3. Data collection and analysis

The data for the study were collected before, during, and after the sessions. Data gathered from the teachers consisted of the teachers' own self-reflective diary, which recorded their experience in terms of choice of FL activities, their adaptation, and implementation. Each teacher reflected on the use of the OER with a view to highlighting its constraints and opportunities in the context of teaching, learning, and changing OEPs.

Both teachers used three sections of the portal, two of which were the search literacy and information literacy sections. The French teacher also drew on visual literacy while the Italian teacher chose to work with filtering literacy. The teachers' reflections on their experience with the tasks were broadly similar and the diaries were investigated adapting the Achieve OER rubrics as follows (https://achieve.org/publications/achieve-oer-rubrics).

### 3.3.1. Degree of alignment of the selected DigiLanguages tasks to the course objectives

The constructive alignment (Biggs, 1996) between the selected tasks on the portal and the course learning outcomes was strong. Each of the tasks includes a general aim, specific learning outcomes, a procedure, and a number of accompanying resources in each language, which aligns with the blueprint for courses, adopted by the two teachers' institution. This eases the process of taking ownership of the OERs. However, both teachers found that the amount of time and effort required to familiarise oneself with the portal's proposed material, structure, and pathways should not be underestimated.

### 3.3.2. Assurance of accessibility

Here we discuss three different levels of accessibility:

- The *materials* did generally not need to be accessed on the portal during class time. When Internet access was required, teachers used the main console or students were asked to use their own devices.

- The *portal's pathways* to the materials did not always appear to be logical. While Dudeney et al.'s (2014) framework provides for a well-structured organisation of DLs, the boundaries between one subset of DLs and another are often pervious and the portal offers a variety of pathways that, despite providing the experienced teacher with a rich choice, may be confusing to a less experienced one. This resulted in one of the teachers missing out on what could have been a relevant activity in the context of information literacy (e.g. an infographics activity placed only under visual literacy and not also under information literacy) or stumbling upon an activity too late in the teaching sequence (e.g. a relevant self-evaluation on digital dependency that could serve as an introductory activity).

- The portal's *accessibility to new contributors* is problematic, as only those who were directly involved with the development of the portal have access to editing its component parts. Ongoing contributions from a broad range of users are currently not feasible, thereby limiting the potential for valuable additions to the portal and raising sustainability concerns.

*3.3.3. Quality of the explanation of the subject matter*

The portal is clearly laid out and the different areas of DLs, with their subsets, are well explained with supporting examples and videos. The CPD sections provide a useful introduction to each of the DLs. The learning outcomes and procedures for the tasks are clearly outlined, despite, at times, either needing some adaptation to meet the particular teaching and learning contexts, or requiring trialling once to fully comprehend the scope of the suggested tasks (e.g. Let's search! activity).

*3.3.4. Utility of the proposed materials designed to support teaching*

The materials in English provided a valuable introduction and overview of the subject matter. The teachers used them only for their own information, mostly due to the fact that they are in English.

The resources made available in the FL tabs for Italian and French were not always reliable in terms of quality and relevance. Some were already outdated, an obsolescence difficult to avoid in the context of the rapidly changing nature of this type of material. In addition, some links are broken and some FL tasks are not fully developed. Such glitches were easily overcome by an experienced teacher, but may be more challenging for inexperienced teachers or teachers whose familiarity with DLs is generally very low.

*3.3.5. Quality of assessment*

The portal does not offer explicit suggestions for assessments. However, task learning outcomes and procedures are generally laid out according to a constructivist view of learning; therefore learners create meaning as they engage with the proposed tasks (Biggs, 1996). In order to successfully carry out the task, following a detailed procedure, students came to understand the issues at stake. The groups being small, high interaction between students themselves and between students and teachers quickly revealed any gaps that needed to be addressed.

*3.3.6. Quality of technological interactivity*

Course design limited technological interactivity as most interactions took place during class time. Preparation of tasks outside of class did not require peer interaction. While the absence of prescribed peer to peer online interaction limits the open pedagogy dimension of this study, teachers found it preferable to acquaint themselves with open pedagogical practices in an incremental manner, thus opting to leverage the potential of online peer collaboration in a subsequent phase of the study.

*3.3.7. Quality of instructional and practice tasks*

The tasks were found to be a very useful means of enhancing FL teachers' practice. For the two teachers who undertook this study, much of their motivation is derived from their direct involvement in the design of the OER and their interest in carrying out research based on the portal.

Teachers who did not participate in the project may not have the same level of interest and determination to invest the time required to use the resource.

*3.3.8. Opportunities for deeper learning*

The proposed tasks encouraged students to analyse and link new practices and concepts to their familiar use of online and social media. Further, the tasks supported students' reflections on the personal significance of DLs in their language learning. The clearly laid out learning outcomes were key in supporting the teachers in adopting new practices with their learners.

## 4. Conclusion

The DigiLanguages OER had a definite positive impact on the teachers' critical reflection in relation to pedagogical practices. Through its development and use, the two teachers became aware of the relevance of embedding DLs in their teaching practice. Also, the portal's rich and accessible material and its potential for fostering deep learning served as an invaluable source of inspiration to implement innovation and changes in their students' learning activities.

Issues related to the time needed to familiarise oneself with the material, to adapt it to one's needs and context, and to deal with the glitches in some of the tasks, however, did not lead to a clear development path for OEP. These issues, often identified in the field (Pegler, 2010; Thoms & Thoms, 2014), might hinder less motivated or more time constrained colleagues who approach the OER. Also, interaction with the resource alone may not be sufficient to encourage colleagues to embed DLs in their practices. This points to the need for teachers' CPD and support for any future implementation. For instance, guidance on integration of DLs within given curricula could usefully be provided at departmental level.

As the DigiLanguages project originated in Ireland, English is the primary language within the portal, and descriptions of DLs as well as of FL tasks are in English, thus restricting its usage for colleagues who understand English.

Finally, the issue of sustainability needs consideration. For security and quality assurance reasons, the portal's updating infrastructure is still a closed system and users are unable to contribute or amend its content. Nevertheless, the portal remains an invaluable resource for any foreign language teacher in higher education institutions.

## Acknowledgements

We would like to thank the Irish National Forum for the Enhancement of Teaching and Learning in Higher Education for funding the DigiLanguages project.

# References

Biggs, J. (1996). Enhancing teaching through constructive alignment. *Higher Education*, *32*(3), 347-364. https://doi.org/10.1007/bf00138871

CEFR. (2001). *Common European framework of reference for languages: learrning, teaching, assessment.* Council of Europe. https://rm.coe.int/16802fc1bf

Dudeney, G., Hockly, N., & Pegrum, M. (2014). *Digital literacies.* Routledge.

European Commission. (2013). *EU high level group: train the professors to teach.* http://europa.eu/rapid/press-release_IP-13-554_en.htm

Irish Department of Education and Skills. (2015). *Digital strategy for schools 2015-2020. Enhancing teaching, learning and assessment.* https://www.education.ie/en/Publications/Policy-Reports/Digital-Strategy-for-Schools-2015-2020.pdf

Karpati, A. (2011). *UNESCO digital literacy in education, policy brief.* http://unesdoc.unesco.org/images/0021/002144/214485e.pdf

Masterman, E., & Wild, J. (2011). *OER impact study: research report.* JISC Open Educational Resources Programme: Phase 2, University of Oxford. https://weblearn.ox.ac.uk/access/content/group/ca5599e6-fd26-4203-b416-f1b96068d1cf/Research%20Project%20Reports/OER%20Projects%202011-2014/JISC%20OER%20Impact%20Study%20Research%20Report%20v1-0.pdf

National Forum. (2015). *Teaching and learning in Irish higher education: a roadmap for enhancement in a digital world 2015-2017.* National Forum for the Enhancement of Teaching and Learning in Higher Education. https://www.teachingandlearning.ie/publication/teaching-and-learning-in-irish-higher-education-a-roadmap-for-enhancement-in-a-digital-world-2015-2017/

Pegler, C. (2010). Building a manifesto for OER sustainability: UK experiences. In *Open Ed 2010 Proceedings.* Barcelona: UOC, OU, BYU. http://hdl.handle.net/10609/5141

Seaman, J. E., & Seaman, J. (2017). *Opening the textbook: educational resources in U.S. Higher Education,* Babson Survey Research Group. https://www.onlinelearningsurvey.com/reports/openingthetextbook2017.pdf

Thoms, J. J., & Thoms, B. L. (2014). Open educational resources in the United States: insights from university foreign language directors. *System*, *45*, 138-146. https://doi.org/10.1016/j.system.2014.05.006

# 5. Learning in the open: integrating language and culture through student curation, virtual exchange, and OER

### Lionel Mathieu[1], Kathryn Murphy-Judy[2], Robert Godwin-Jones[3], Laura Middlebrooks[4], and Natalia Boykova[5]

## Abstract

To address waning enrollments in intermediate 202 language courses, faculty have developed a multiphasic project. In phase one, alongside instructional designers, they created an open, connected platform where 202 students curate – search, select, and share – authentic materials online. In phase two, upper-level students help triage and scaffold the best curations into online interactive modules. Phase three sets up live, virtual exchanges during which students discuss their curations with native speakers. In phase four, open e-textbooks, framed by communicative can-do statements, integrate curations, modules, virtual exchanges, and existing Open Educational Resources (OERs) into sustainable, relevant, and student driven learning materials.

Keywords: OER, digital literacy, curation, virtual exchange.

---

1. Boston University, Boston, Massachusetts, United States; lmathieu@bu.edu

2. Virginia Commonwealth University, Richmond, Virginia, United States; kmurphy@vcu.edu; https://orcid.org/0000-0002-6706-731X

3. Virginia Commonwealth University, Richmond, Virginia, United States; rgjones@vcu.edu; https://orcid.org/0000-0002-2377-3204

4. Virginia Commonwealth University, Richmond, Virginia, United States; middlebrooks@vcu.edu

5. Virginia Commonwealth University, Richmond, Virginia, United States; nvboykova@vcu.edu

How to cite this chapter: Mathieu, L., Murphy-Judy, K., Godwin-Jones, R., Middlebrooks, L., & Boykova, N. (2019). Learning in the open: integrating language and culture through student curation, virtual exchange, and OER. In A. Comas-Quinn, A. Beaven & B. Sawhill (Eds), *New case studies of openness in and beyond the language classroom* (pp. 65-82). Research-publishing.net. https://doi.org/10.14705/rpnet.2019.37.967

Chapter 5

## 1. Context of the project

American colleges and universities are suffering declining enrollments in world languages (Looney & Lusin, 2018). Nevertheless, a report by the Language Flagship Technology Innovation Center at the University of Hawaii offers an encouraging vision of foreign language education: "institutions are emphasizing more active, real-world experiences that better equip students for responsible global citizenship and successful participation in professional and interpersonal communicative contexts" (Adams Becker, Rodriguez, Estrada, & Davis, 2016, p.1). It also reminds us that "[l]anguage education, by nature, is a multi-year endeavor. It requires dedication from students outside of the classroom to fully realize the unique contexts of specific words, phrases, and semiotic actions in other cultures" (Adams Becker et al., 2016, p.1). Finally, the report states that technologies that facilitate personalization and faculty development to work with such advances, are just now emerging. This project attempts to align with such a vision of student-centered, authentic language education.

In 2015, language faculty at Virginia Commonwealth University (VCU) identified a roadblock: the second semester of the second-year (202). Most students stop language study, expressing disappointment at their inability to communicate well in the target language. These same students, however, are highly engaged in digital communication and demonstrate a keen interest in social connections. Our task, then, was to get them to pursue language study by connecting it to their 'real' lives.

## 2. Intended outcomes

This multiphasic project connects student language learning with engaging, digital communications. Through online curation – the searching, selecting, and sharing – of target language resources, students discover personal learning paths through course themes and structures. Final curations relate language learning to future aspirations and personal interests. Students who participate in selecting learning materials show greater personal investment in learning (Oxford et al.,

2014). It also develops self-evaluation skills and critical literacy, two crucial competencies today (Warner & Dupuy, 2018). Curating provides the class with authentic materials. Those chosen as scaffolded modules loop back into the learning program. Through virtual exchanges, students explore their curations with native speakers in real time, developing linguistic and cultural acumen. The project targets digital literacy, autonomous language learning, and global citizenry.

The project continues to evolve. It began with faculty and students learning to curate. At the end of each year, upper-level students help triage curations for interest and pedagogical promise. Those become scaffolded modules for class use. Since Year 2, virtual exchanges have been added to deepen student interpretive and interpersonal communication with curated content. Most recently, the team has embarked on the creation of OER e-textbooks that weave together all facets of the project – with students and their learning squarely in the center of both process and product. What follows showcases various realizations of the desired learning outcomes, with glimpses into each phase of the process. The supplementary materials section provides student reactions to the curation phase of their learning and comments by the student researchers on co-creating modules and the OER e-textbooks with faculty.

## 3. Nuts and bolts

### 3.1. Student curation of authentic materials

The first phase of the project asks intermediate-level students to locate online resources, documents, and/or artifacts produced by the target language community for its own use and consumption. We refer to such digital finds as *authentic materials*, as they are generated by and intended for a native audience. Language collected from authentic media provides a counterpoint to the often artificial language presented in textbooks (Gilmore, 2007). Language textbooks

> "'have become more and more like tourist brochures' (Kramsch, 2014, p. 308), with glossy photos, stereotypical topics, and quickly outdated

## Chapter 5

information. [...] Textbooks typically do not provide exposure to the evolving array of online genres for reading and writing. [...] This is particularly problematic at a time in which most of the reading and writing in our students' personal and professional lives will be online (Chun, Kern, & Smith, 2016)" (Godwin-Jones, 2018b, p. 146).

Typical second-year course thematics (e.g. travel, city life, environmental issues, politics, etc.) frame the topics that students research and collate, some of which may later be used to support online modules (see section 2 below). Faculty members have worked with instructional designers to create an open and connected curation platform[6] where students syndicate their finds, as well as learn aspects of digital information retrieval and manipulation (e.g. categorization/tagging, syndication/aggregation, and copyright/copyleft). The platform offers written instructions as well as video tutorials for students to set up their accounts (Figure 1), guide the selection and curation processes (Figure 2), and articulate a narrative about the submitted materials in the target language.

Figure 1.  Instructions for setting up student accounts in WordPress

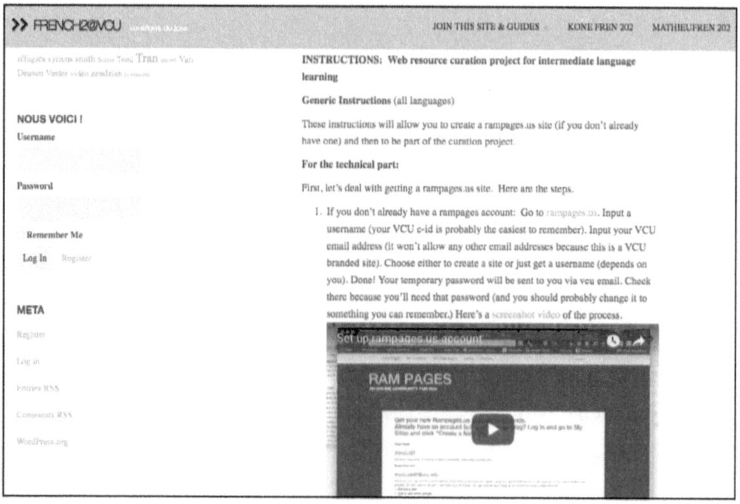

---

6. Language-specific curation platforms: rampages.us/french2atvcu, rampages.us/chinese2atvcu, rampages.us/russian2atvcu, rampages.us/spanish2atvcu, rampages.us/italian2atvcu, rampages.us/german2atvcu.

Figure 2.  Instructions for curating: part of the student guide

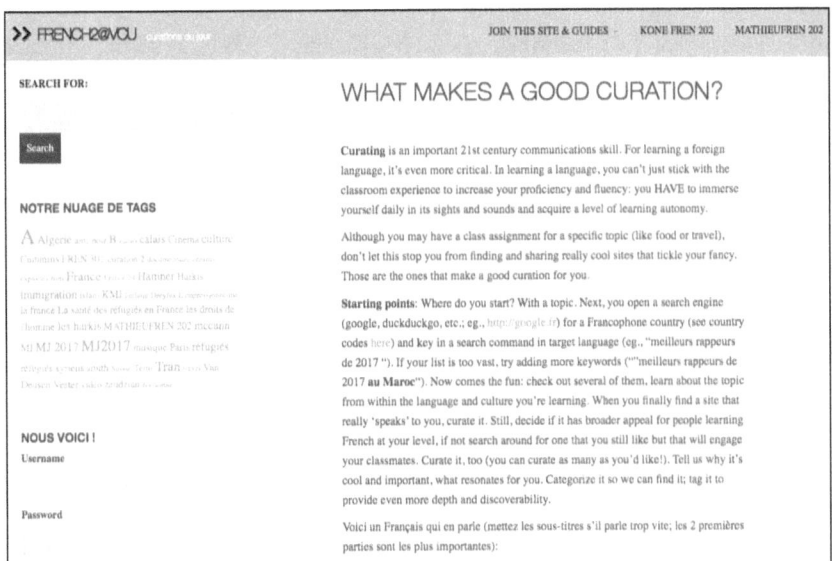

Each student is asked to find and curate a prescribed number of online documents or sites, and write a short paragraph or two accounting for the source and nature of the selected document(s) (text, video, ad, blog post, news article, etc.), as well as a rationale for the selection. Students learning the same world language are also able to see their peers' submissions and rate them using a five star scale (Figure 3). This feature has proven to be particularly valuable when determining the merit of these documents as the basis for selection as online modules (see section 2 below).

Students now curate for their professional aspirations, connecting language learning with future careers in sciences, arts, commerce, etc. to promote language acquisition beyond formal instruction. Because many of our students are destined to join professional fields where knowledge of another language may not be foregrounded in the US, increasing awareness of and exposure to a multilingual world may persuade some to view linguistic capital as an asset worth continued investment (see the supplementary materials). Some students

## Chapter 5

may not readily see the value in pursuing language study, but envisioning themselves in a "community in which [they] might belong and use the information [they] are learning" (Murphey, Chen, & Chen, 2005, p. 98) may encourage them toward more meaningful, ongoing participation in learning (Norton, 2001).

Figure 3. Annotated screenshot of the loading page of rampages.us/french2atvcu as instructional guide

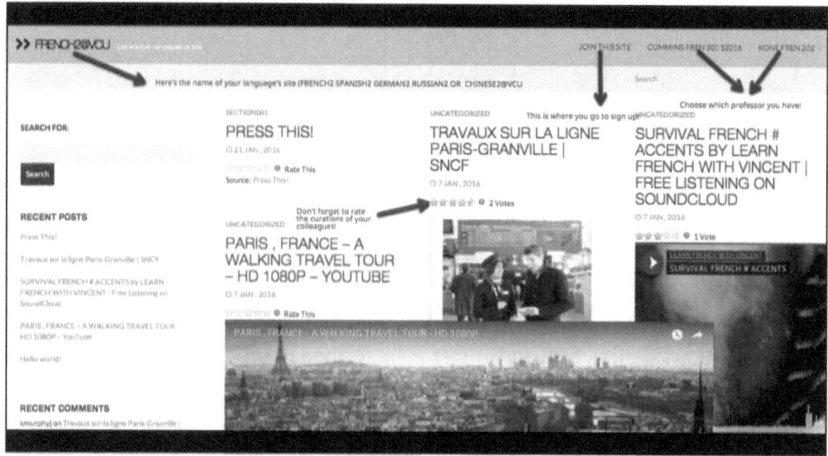

### 3.2. Student OER module co-creation and design

The second phase of the project recruits advanced students to work with faculty to select highly rated, pedagogically valuable curations from the current corpus. Given the volume of submissions from the curation phase, the student-faculty team first establishes a set of criteria (based on textbook thematics, students' ratings, and cultural and linguistic pertinence) to narrow down the stock of materials for possible online module creation. In language teams, we then scaffold the vetted, authentic media so as to guide the intermediate learners through linguistically and culturally appropriate interpretations and knowledge. Student researchers work with faculty members to devise these supportive learning environments, relying on OER and interactive tools[7] (for instance, H5P[8] for interactivity).

We initially started with one undergraduate student per language, but within the span of a year, some languages were able to recruit more. Various opportunities enable advanced students to partake in this phase of the project by way of university-internal grants or assorted independent study courses. Undergraduate research and experiential learning is a hallmark of a VCU education and better prepares students for their respective careers[9]. For these students, working in tandem with a faculty member means increased exposure to and performance in the target language beyond what a typical classroom offers. Ultimately, the modules show how to navigate authentic texts on one's own, regardless of the context and with guidance toward more critical reading and greater intercultural sensitivity (see the supplementary materials for student testimonials on module co-creation and design).

One Spanish-language module[10] serves here as an example of content development appropriate for intermediate-level instruction. As part of the initial phase of authentic materials collection, a fourth semester student curated on the scientific benefits of napping, a culturally important aspect of daily Spanish life, and uploaded it to the curation website to share with classmates. In the second phase, a Spanish program faculty member mentored two advanced-level students about potential pedagogical applications of such an article. In particular, the advanced students learned about the value of both pre-reading activities (to engage readers by applying their background knowledge to the topic), and post-reading activities (to check comprehension and provide an opportunity to write personal reflections in the target language). The advanced students, applying this new knowledge, created exercises that

---

7. Examples of language-specific modules: Chinese module: https://rampages.us/chineseoer/modules/moi/; French module: https://rampages.us/frenchoer/modules/je-veux/, https://rampages.us/frenchoer/modules/menace-de-mort-youssoupha/; Italian module: https://rampages.us/italianoer/modules/tradizioni/; Russian module: https://rampages.us/russianoer/modules/голобой-вагон-и-возвратных-глаголов/

8. See https://h5p.org

9. See https://provost.vcu.edu/academic-affairs/real/

10. See Spanish Module https://rampages.us/spanishoer/modules/los-beneficios-de-la-siesta/

encourage intermediate-level students to (1) read strategically for vocabulary comprehension, (2) promote their understanding of the article, and (3) deploy the newly-acquired vocabulary to their lives as sleep-deprived college students (Figure 4). For example, the pre-reading vocabulary task includes culturally and physiologically important verbs and phrases (e.g. *padecer*=to suffer (e.g. insomnia), *echar una siesta*=to take a nap, and *las alteraciones del sueño*=sleep changes). A post-reading activity quizzes students about the health benefits of a good night's sleep with true/false questions like *¿La siesta reduce el grado de estrés y las tensiones físicas?* (do naps reduce stress and physical tension?). Finally, the advanced students created a series of questions that range from very short ones like *¿Usted las toma?, ¿Con qué frecuencia?* (do you take naps? How frequently?) to more open-ended queries about students' sleep habits, like *¿Cómo se siente después de tomarlas?* (how do you feel after a nap?). In this particular module, each question is designed to elicit specific structures with which the average intermediate student still struggles (direct object pronouns, reflexive verbs, and use of infinitives with prepositions).

Figure 4. Screenshot of an OER module on the benefits of *siestas* with interactive reading

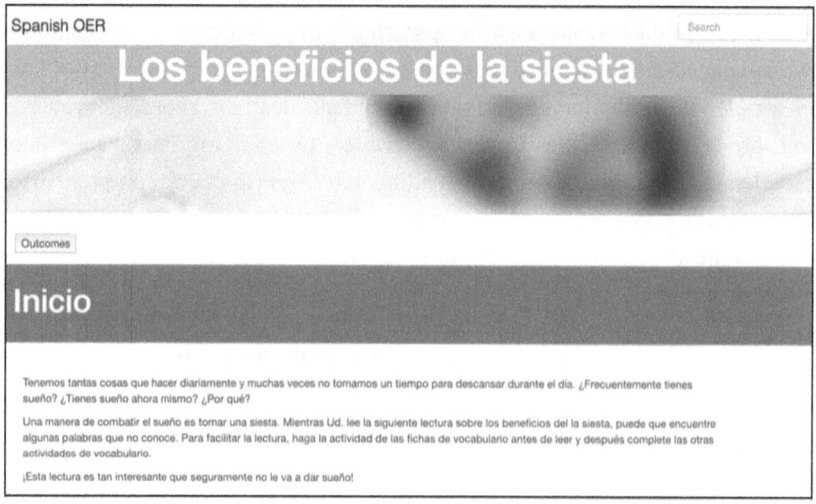

The next stage of our ongoing project is to fully integrate these learner-generated modules into language courseware delivered via open e-textbooks. Again, upper division students contribute significantly to this effort by co-creating materials alongside faculty members. Thus, they are engaging in 'participatory action research' (Zuber-Skerrit, 2002), helping to find and create materials likely to be of interest to their peers.

### 3.3. Student virtual exchanges with native speakers

To complement students' experiences of curating authentic materials in their target language, two virtual exchange formats have been introduced: Teletandem[11], an online exchange program that partners students with peers at overseas institutions of higher learning, and Talk Abroad[12], a private company that partners students with paid native tutors in target countries. The addition of this component to the curation part of the project enables intermediate-level students to participate in a community of native speakers with a high reality quotient since the conversations revolve around their curations. It allows students to appreciate, explore, grasp, and navigate both the linguistic and cultural content of their curated documents directly with a native informant (see the supplementary materials for student testimonials on virtual exchange)[13].

In the VCU Russian language program, for instance, Teletandem has allowed VCU students to communicate with their peers at Moscow State University since 2013 (Figure 5), and with Moscow Pedagogical University students since 2016. These online exchanges are particularly well suited to the study of foreign languages because students have the chance to communicate with native speakers over the course of the semester through synchronous online interactions. Such an arrangement is highly effective in providing students with authentic and meaningful opportunities for immersion and practice in their respective second language, even more so when the partners are discussing an

---

11. https://media.worldstudies.vcu.edu/teletandem/what-is-teletandem/

12. https://talkabroad.com

13. See this YouTube video of a French student engaging with his Belgian teletandem partner in a negotiation of meaning over the concept of a 'food desert': https://youtu.be/JD3-6Qd_5_E

interesting curation. Students are motivated to practice new vocabulary, forms, and ideas drawn from their research and to explore cultural factors coloring their interpretation of the curated media. It thus widens their cultural knowledge and makes them reflect on their own language and societal norms, increasing their intercultural competence.

Figure 5.  Russian 202 class interacting with Moscow State University students via Teletandem

In the Talk Abroad venue, a paid service, each student benefits from either 10 or 30 minute live sessions over the course of the semester. Upon registering on the site, students first select a speaking partner, listed by country of residence along with a short biographical profile, and subsequently schedule their conversational sessions at their own convenience. Overlooking some initial apprehension at the prospect of interacting with a native speaker (an unfamiliar exercice for most intermediate-level students), at the end of spring 2018, the majority of students surveyed expressed a genuine appreciation for this challenging yet rewarding and empowering task. One or more of the Talk Abroad sessions are designed to elicit discussion of student curations so that learners can expand their linguistic and cultural interpretation of their chosen authentic materials. One student, for instance, relied on a curated article about the use of henna in Tunisian weddings to connect with her Talk Abroad partner from Tunisia and enrich her understanding of that cultural practice, all the while aptly maneuvering across some uncharted linguistic terrains. During these audiovisual interactions, students often manage to go beyond rudimentary conversational routines to deploy concrete conversational strategies (such as circumlocution of linguistic gaps, negotiation of turn-taking and communication breakdowns, topical shifts, and maintenance) to achieve meaning-making usages of language. In sum, in addition to fostering their grammatical and sociolinguistic competence, students also actively engage in developing a nascent 'strategic competence' (Canale & Swain, 1980) in their second language.

### 3.4. Merit of the project

This multifaceted project in world languages offers a dynamic framework for students to develop appropriate intermediate-level language skills capable of sustaining more advanced language acquisition. With a committed focus on students' academics, personal interests, and professional lives, it aims to provide them with a critical foundation in meaningful language study and growth. In essence, this project endeavors to encourage student enthusiasm for continuing investment in language study, whether in or out of the classroom environment. Chief among the merits of the project, are:

- **Engaging students across the language curriculum.** From the curation of authentic materials by intermediate-level students to the co-creation of online modules by advanced-level students, the project is inherently learner-driven yet supported by faculty expertise and oversight. Furthermore, attention to students' interests and professional aspirations personalizes language study far beyond the mass-market textbook, thereby granting students ownership of their language education.

- **Language study via discovery learning, fostering a spirit of inquiry and learner autonomy.** The intrinsically exploratory nature of the curation and virtual exchange parts of the project enable students to uncover a world of non-English products, practices, and perspectives, broadening their horizons, and enriching their intercultural competence. By tapping into students' interests, this project nourishes intellectual curiosity and professional ambitions, all the while fostering their ability to learn autonomously.

- **Enhancing digital literacy and skills.** Twenty-first century students are immersed in a world of readily-accessible information, yet, digital natives appear to grapple with the ability to discern the validity or veracity of that information critically (Wineburg, McGrew, Breakstone, & Ortega, 2016). By learning to curate and justify their choice of certain documents, students engage in deeper reflection about the texts and their sources that they encounter. Curating, after all, is information gathering and sorting. Likewise, by appraising the pedagogical value of various second language curations, advanced students develop an intellectual acuity for interpreting foreign digital design and content.

- **Sustaining meaningful language learning activity (in and out of the classroom).** Disenfranchisement in second language learners is commonplace, especially at the intermediate-level, when students' proficiency levels tend to plateau (Gass & Selinker, 2008). Only by providing genuine opportunities to practice language skills authentically (e.g. reading and writing via curations; listening and speaking via virtual exchanges) can faculty hope to instill interest in further language acquisition.

- **Developing relevant, current, and affordable OER course content.** The growing use of and reliance on open access multimedia compels educators to reflect on the value of static, expensive, proprietary materials like traditional textbooks, however much they may be modernized by technological bells and whistles. Although relatively young, the OER movement increasingly challenges traditional educational practices and materials while emerging studies indicate that OERs perform as well instructionally, if not better, than traditional ones for student learning and engagement (Weller et al., 2015). Recent studies of OER use have indicated that student reception is positive, with students appreciating the lower cost, but also the option of content customization (Hilton, 2016). This project aims to create modular OER textbooks, enabling others to use only those modules or e-book chapters that fit personal or curricular needs (Dixon & Hondo, 2014).

In its focus on encouraging both language and cultural competency, this project aligns with recent emphases in second language acquisition research on the responsibility of language educators to also help students develop a sense of global citizenship (Byram, Golubeva, Hui, & Wagner, 2017; Hennebry, 2017; Warner & Dupuy, 2018) and to encourage them to find ways to integrate language learning into contributions to the social good (Dasli & Diaz, 2016; Larsen-Freeman, 2018). The recent inclusion of the LinguaFolio e-portfolio (based on the European model) as the pedagogical and proficiency based framework for the development of the e-textbooks aligns with the emphasis on student responsibility for reflection, engagement, and autonomy, with students charting their own progress and targeting their own learning goals (Little, 2009; Moeller, Theiler, & Wu, 2012; Moeller & Yu, 2015; Ziegler, 2014).

## 4. Conclusion

This project aims to encourage and enable American students to become engaged language learners and digital global citizens, appreciative of other cultures, and knowledgeable about opportunities for continued language study. The hope is that a substantial number of students engaged in the project will continue their target language study formally or informally. Increasingly, the latter is becoming the norm (Godwin-Jones, 2018a; Kusyk, 2017). These online resources will likely be the means for most students to connect language learning with their future professional lives. While that is already integrated into the curation process, the language team plans to reach out to professional units of the university to explore collaborative opportunities. The importance of knowledge of a second language across disciplines is delineated in a 2017 report published by the Commission on Language Learning at the American Academy of Arts and Sciences (2017)[14].

Another anticipated direction for the project is integration into university-sponsored study abroad programs. Teletandem and Talk Abroad participation

---

14. See https://www.amacad.org/project/commission-language-learning

may serve to enhance student interest in directly experiencing the target culture. That might occur through individual initiative but could also lead to participation in organized study abroad. Research has shown that creation and use of locally developed language resources geared to study abroad locales increases participation in programs as well as in student enrollment in language study (Goertler, 2015). There is also the opportunity for students abroad to contribute to the project themselves by filming local resources, conducting short interviews, or engaging in other means of gathering and curating language/culture-related materials (Godwin-Jones, 2017). This encourages students abroad to think of themselves as ethnographers, chronicling and reflecting on personal experiences in the target culture (Roberts, 2001). Of course, participation by students in the project in itself should prove helpful in building linguistic and cultural competence that will be beneficial to study, work, or leisure abroad. Thanks to two student research funds, we currently have two students, one in Russian and one in French, contributing their experiences and research abroad into modules for the e-textbooks.

Finally, second language learning is especially important in largely monolingual cultures like the US, where only 25% of 'mainstream' Americans have studied a foreign language at some point in their lives (Devlin, 2015) and only 20% of students at the secondary level enroll in language classes (American Councils for International Education, 2017). As Ortega (2017) remarks, this has had an unfortunate by-product in terms of acceptance of diversity in the US: "It is in great part marginalized monolinguals who are blamed for the rise of authoritarian populism in the West and the disaffection for human solidarity and human diversity ideals" (p. 308). Foreign language study creates more positive attitudes toward those who are different, a much-needed orientation throughout the world today.

## Acknowledgments

We would like to express our thanks to our colleague in Italian, Dr Vera Abbate, for her unfaltering dedication and hard work, to Tom Woodward, Associate

Director, Learning Innovation, for his unwavering support in all technical aspects of this project, to the VCU Undergraduate Research Opportunity Program, the Faculty Council of the College of Humanities and Sciences, the Global Education Office Virtual Classroom Grant, VCU Libraries Affordable Course Content Awards, and the Baldacci Scholarship for granting us and our student researchers financial support to carry out this innovative enterprise in language learning and teaching, and to our world language colleagues for their open mindedness and cooperation as we blaze new trails in world language pedagogy. Last, but certainly not least, we are grateful to all the students involved in any part of this project: your participation and enthusiasm are what makes this project worth pursuing and are paramount to its success.

## Supplementary materials

https://research-publishing.box.com/s/o86o6t87wildyvjsr4etvkr4in6j9bt8

## References

Adams Becker, S., Rodriguez, J. C., Estrada, V., & Davis, A. (2016). Innovating language education: an NMC Horizon project strategic brief (Volume 3.1). The New Media Consortium. http://cdn.nmc.org/media/2016-nmc-strategic-brief-language_ed.pdf

American Academy of Arts & Sciences. (2017). America's languages: investing in language education for the 21st Century. https://www.amacad.org/content/Research/researchproject.aspx?d=21896

American Councils for International Education. (2017). *The National K–12 foreign language enrollment survey, 2017*. American Councils for International Education, American Council for the Teaching of Foreign Languages, & Center for Applied Linguistics.

Byram, M., Golubeva, I., Hui, H., & Wagner, M. (Eds). (2017). *From principles to practice in education for intercultural citizenship*. Multilingual Matters. https://doi.org/10.21832/9781783096565

Canale, M., & Swain, M. (1980). Theoretical bases of communicative approaches to second language teaching and testing. *Applied Linguistics, 7*(1), 1-47.

Chun, D., Kern, R., & Smith, B. (2016). Technology in language use, language teaching, and language learning. *Modern Language Journal, 100*(S1), 64-80. https://doi.org/10.1111/modl.12302

Dasli, M., & Diaz, A. R. (Eds). (2016). *The critical turn in language and intercultural communication pedagogy: theory, research and practice*. Routledge. https://doi.org/10.4324/9781315667294

Devlin, K. (2015, July 13). *Learning a foreign language a 'must' in Europe, not so in America*. Pew Research Center.

Dixon, E. M., & Hondo, J. (2014). Re-purposing an OER for the online language course: a case study of Deutsch Interaktiv by the Deutsche Welle. *Computer Assisted Language Learning, 27*(2), 109-121. https://doi.org/10.1080/09588221.2013.818559

Gass, S. M., & Selinker, L. (2008). Second language acquisition, an introductory course (3rd ed.). Lawrence Erlbaum Associates.

Gilmore, A. (2007). Authentic materials and authenticity in foreign language learning. *Language teaching, 40*(2), 97-118. https://doi.org/10.1017/s0261444807004144

Godwin-Jones, R. (2017). Smartphones and language learning. *Language Learning & Technology, 21*(2), 3-17.

Godwin-Jones, R. (2018a). Chasing the butterfly effect: informal language learning online as a complex system. *Language Learning & Technology, 22*(2), 8-27.

Godwin-Jones, R. (2018b). Restructuring intermediate language instruction with open and student-curated materials. CALL your DATA, Proceedings Brugge, KULeuven & imec 4-6 July 2018 (pp. 144-151). https://www.call2018.org/wp-content/uploads/2018/07/proceedings-CALL-2018.pdf?

Goertler, S. (2015, July 13). *Study abroad and technology: friend or enemy?* http://fltmag.com/study-abroad-and-technology/

Hennebry, M. (2017). Foreign language teaching for citizenship development. In S. Coffey & U. Wingate (Eds), (2017). *New directions for research in foreign language education*. Routledge. https://doi.org/10.4324/9781315561561-4

Hilton, J. (2016). Open educational resources and college textbook choices: a review of research on efficacy and perceptions. *Educational Technology Research and Development, 64*(4), 573-590. https://doi.org/10.1007/s11423-016-9434-9

Kramsch, C. (2014). Teaching foreign languages in an era of globalization: introduction. *The Modern Language Journal, 98*(1), 296-311. https://doi.org/10.1111/j.1540-4781.2014.12057.x

Kusyk, M. (2017). The development of complexity, accuracy, and fluency in L2 written production through informal participation in online activities. *CALICO Journal, 34*(1), 75-96. https://doi.org/10.1558/cj.29513

Larsen-Freeman, D. (2018). Looking ahead: future directions in, and future research into, second language acquisition. *Foreign Language Annals, 51*(1), 55-72. https://doi.org/10.1111/flan.12314

Little, D. (2009). Language learner autonomy and the European language portfolio: two L2 English examples. *Language Teaching, 42*(2), 222-233. https://doi.org/10.1017/s0261444808005636

Looney, D., & Lusin, N. (2018). Enrollments in languages other than English in United States institutions of higher education (web version). Modern Language Association of America. https://www.mla.org/content/download/83540/2197676/2016-Enrollments-Short-Report.pdf

Moeller, A., Theiler, J., & Wu, C. (2012). Goal setting and student achievement: a longitudinal study. *The Modern Language Journal, 96*(2), 153-169. https://doi.org/10.1111/j.1540-4781.2011.01231.x

Moeller, A., & Yu, F. (2015). NCSSFL-ACTFL can-do statements: an effective tool for improving language learning within and outside the classroom. In P. Swanson (Ed.), Dimension 2015 (pp. 50-69). SCOLT.

Murphey, T., Chen, J., & Chen, L. (2005). Learners' constructions of identities and imagined communities. In P. Benson & D. Nunan, (Eds). *Learners' stories: difference and diversity in language learning* (pp. 83-100). Cambridge University Press.

Norton, B. (2001). Non-participation, imagined communities, and the language classroom. In M. Breen (Ed.), *Learner contributions to language learning: new directions in research* (pp. 159-171). Pearson.

Ortega, L. (2017). New CALL-SLA research interfaces for the 21st century: towards equitable multilingualism. *CALICO journal, 34*(3), 285-316. https://doi.org/10.1558/cj.33855

Oxford, R. L., Rubin, J., Chamot, A. U., Schramm, K., Lavine, R., Gunning, P., & Nel, C. (2014). The learning strategy prism: perspectives of learning strategy experts. *System, 43*, 30-49. https://doi.org/10.1016/j.system.2014.02.004

Roberts, C. (2001). *Language learners as ethnographers*. Multilingual Matters.

Warner, C., & Dupuy, B. (2018). Moving toward multiliteracies in foreign language teaching: past and present perspectives... and beyond. *Foreign Language Annals, 51*(1), 116-128. https://doi.org/10.1111/flan.12316

Weller, M., de los Arcos, B., Farrow, R., Pitt, B., & McAndrew, P. (2015). The Impact of OER on teaching and learning practice. *Open Praxis, 7*(4), 351-361. https://doi.org/10.5944/openpraxis.7.4.227

Wineburg, S., McGrew, S., Breakstone, J., & Ortega, T. (2016). *Evaluating information: the cornerstone of civic online reasoning.* Stanford Digital Repository. http://purl.stanford.edu/fv751yt5934

Ziegler, N. (2014). Fostering self-regulated learning through the European language portfolio: an intervention mixed methods study. *The Modern Language Journal, 98*(4), 921- 936. https://doi.org/10.1111/modl.12147

Zuber-Skerrit, O. (2002). A model for designing action learning and action research programs *The Learning Organisation, 9*(4), 143-149. https://doi.org/10.1108/09696470210428868

# Section 2.
# Working in open spaces

# 6. Building bridges not walls – Wikipedia in Translation Studies

## Ewan McAndrew[1] and Lorna Campbell[2]

### Abstract

Translation Studies MSc students at the University of Edinburgh take part in a Wikipedia translation assignment as part of their independent study component. The students make use of the free and open encyclopaedia's Content Translation tool which enables them to create translations side-by-side to the original article and automates the process of formatting the page. By providing a more user-friendly experience, translators can focus on creating high-quality content that reads naturally and fluently. Course leaders were keen that the students undertake much-needed published translation practice each semester to bridge the gap between academic study and the world of work ahead of their dissertations. This chapter explains how the project was structured and delivered.

Keywords: Wikipedia, translation, University of Edinburgh, content translation.

## 1. Context of the project

"Wikipedia is about building bridges, not walls" (Wales, 2016).

Translation Studies is a one-year, full-time taught Masters programme at the University of Edinburgh which aims to enhance "practical skills in, and

---

1. University of Edinburgh, Edinburgh, Scotland; ewan.mcandrew@ed.ac.uk

2. University of Edinburgh, Edinburgh, Scotland; lorna.m.campbell@ed.ac.uk; https://orcid.org/0000-0001-6767-856X

How to cite this chapter: McAndrew, E., & Campbell, L. (2019). Building bridges not walls – Wikipedia in Translation Studies. In A. Comas-Quinn, A. Beaven & B. Sawhill (Eds), *New case studies of openness in and beyond the language classroom* (pp. 85-100). Research-publishing.net. https://doi.org/10.14705/rpnet.2019.37.968

theoretical understanding of, translation as an activity" (The University of Edinburgh, 2019a, n.p.). Between 2016/2017 and 2018/2019, 20 to 30 students registered annually in the Translation Studies MSc, which supports a wide variety of languages (Arabic, Chinese, Danish, French, German, Japanese, Norwegian, Spanish, Swedish, and Turkish in 2018/2019.

The Wikipedia assignment is an elective component of the programme's independent study course, which runs as a semester-long assignment in the first and second semesters. Students are free to choose which language pair they work in but are encouraged to change language direction in Semester 2. The students are supported by the University of Edinburgh's 'Wikimedian in residence'; a digital skills trainer employed by the university's information services division in partnership with, and supported by, Wikimedia UK as the national chapter of the non-profit Wikimedia Foundation. The residency is a free service to support staff and students to learn about, contribute to, and benefit from the Wikimedia Foundation's family of Open Knowledge projects, of which Wikipedia, the free and open encyclopaedia, is by far the best known. The assignment came about as a result of a practical translation workshop at the Wikimedia Foundation's annual conference, Wikimania, held in Esino Lario in Summer 2016. During the workshop, the University of Edinburgh's Wikimedian in residence, Ewan McAndrew, was introduced to Wikipedia's Content Translation tool, which is designed to better enable knowledge exchange by taking the headache out of formatting pages when translating between different language Wikipedias. The Wikimedian in residence shared this knowledge with course leaders on the Translation Studies MSc, who agreed to trial a Wikipedia translation assignment on the course programme in the first semester of the 2016/2017 academic year. This assignment has continued for the last six semesters.

## 2. Intended outcomes

The formatively assessed independent study course is intended to give students much-needed authentic translation experience of 2,000-4,000 words each semester before they enter the world of work. Course leaders were keen to motivate students to complete this translation practice as it was a core objective of the Masters programme. The prospect of the students being able to actually *publish* their work online as a clearly demonstrable and lasting output of their studies, as well as one that could be added to and improved over time as a community project, was thought to be a great opportunity in keeping with the University of Edinburgh's (2019b) vision "to make a significant, sustainable and socially responsible contribution to the world" (n.p.).

A study by Selwyn and Gorard (2016) found that 87.5% of students were finding Wikipedia 'academically useful' in an introductory or clarificatory role. Course leaders were mindful that students were *already* using Wikipedia and therefore should be supported in developing good habits in terms of the necessary digital research skills ahead of undertaking their dissertation.

Wikipedia is the largest reference work on the internet, with 49 million articles in 302 different languages. Google's algorithm ranks Wikipedia articles so they routinely appear in the first page of search results. There is real agency to Wikipedia editing in terms of being able to surface knowledge between different languages and cultures. Addressing areas of underrepresentation and building understanding between different languages is particularly important when one considers how unevenly knowledge is spread between the approximately 302 different language Wikipedias (see Figure 1 below).

Following recent Wikipedia translation projects elsewhere (Al-Shehari, 2017; Martínez Carrasco, 2018), this Wikipedia translation assignment was introduced to help motivate a diverse group of Masters students, working on a wide range of language combinations, to translate 2,000 words individually in each semester. The objective was to let them see the value of sharing their scholarship in a published context as a significant and demonstrable output of their studies that would last beyond the life of the assignment. This chapter further evidences how moving to a student-centred learning environment can improve motivation and further explores how "introducing collaborative projects with genuine outcomes, we can allow students to coherently develop the competences required for professional translators" (Al-Shehari, 2017, p. 371).

Chapter 6

Figure 1.  Screenshot excerpt from the List of Wikipedias in March 2019[3]

| Language | Language (local) | Wiki | Articles | Total | Edits | Admins | Users | Active users | Images | Depth |
|---|---|---|---|---|---|---|---|---|---|---|
| English | English | en | 5,817,966 | 47,283,382 | 881,932,743 | 1,181 | 35,837,865 | 141,047 | 881,615 | 947.45 |
| Cebuano | Cebuano | ceb | 5,379,102 | 9,087,479 | 25,633,974 | 6 | 56,028 | 181 | 0 | 1.34 |
| Swedish | svenska | sv | 3,751,809 | 7,701,516 | 45,135,306 | 66 | 660,377 | 2,813 | 0 | 6.5 |
| German | Deutsch | de | 2,279,339 | 6,392,173 | 185,121,871 | 189 | 3,138,185 | 20,448 | 129,451 | 94.29 |
| French | français | fr | 2,086,956 | 10,048,896 | 156,864,382 | 157 | 3,380,333 | 19,413 | 57,305 | 227.2 |
| Dutch | Nederlands | nl | 1,959,911 | 4,059,675 | 53,183,907 | 44 | 980,934 | 4,323 | 22 | 15.04 |
| Russian | русский | ru | 1,533,261 | 5,831,384 | 98,213,350 | 84 | 2,483,999 | 11,977 | 216,029 | 132.35 |
| Italian | italiano | it | 1,511,695 | 6,121,983 | 102,869,792 | 111 | 1,792,104 | 8,799 | 140,079 | 156.29 |
| Spanish | español | es | 1,509,273 | 6,599,133 | 113,972,121 | 73 | 5,345,110 | 16,998 | 0 | 196.42 |
| Polish | polski | pl | 1,323,172 | 2,984,382 | 55,886,431 | 103 | 944,189 | 4,588 | 265 | 29.52 |
| Waray | Winaray | war | 1,263,531 | 2,877,124 | 6,197,874 | 3 | 39,479 | 86 | 42 | 3.51 |
| Vietnamese | Tiếng Việt | vi | 1,203,627 | 14,481,130 | 50,198,752 | 21 | 653,533 | 1,741 | 30,179 | 421.83 |
| Japanese | 日本語 | ja | 1,142,242 | 3,383,476 | 71,704,601 | 42 | 1,451,631 | 13,808 | 85,376 | 81.59 |
| Chinese | 中文 | zh | 1,048,137 | 5,702,234 | 53,181,011 | 80 | 2,691,937 | 8,061 | 51,087 | 183.89 |
| Portuguese | português | pt | 1,018,719 | 4,798,116 | 54,266,590 | 81 | 2,219,321 | 5,631 | 51,622 | 155.57 |
| Ukrainian | українська | uk | 891,048 | 2,689,912 | 24,549,960 | 45 | 444,514 | 3,303 | 98,954 | 37.2 |
| Arabic | العربية | ar | 704,453 | 4,566,995 | 33,444,179 | 29 | 1,632,204 | 4,392 | 32,422 | 220.16 |
| Persian | فارسی | fa | 668,474 | 4,294,017 | 25,595,448 | 33 | 807,083 | 5,089 | 55,055 | 175.34 |

## 3. Nuts and bolts

### 3.1. Setting the context – empowering language activism

Two workshops at the beginning of the semester were facilitated by the Wikimedian in residence. The first workshop session introduces the students to the work of the Wikimedia Foundation, Wikipedia's main policies and guidelines, and how to create a user page using Wikipedia's new easy-to-use What-You-See-Is-What-You-Get (WYSIWYG) visual editor interface. Next, the Content Translation tool must be enabled using the beta menu at the top right of any Wikipedia page (see Figure 2 below).

The first workshop closes with best practice on how to select a good article to work on so students can select one ahead of the next workshop. The students must *each* produce a translation of 2,000 words but can decide whether they will work individually, in pairs, or in groups to achieve this. They choose the

---

3. https://en.wikipedia.org/wiki/List_of_Wikipedias

language pair and subject matter, which should be one that interests them and will benefit readers when the translation is published.

Figure 2. Enabling content translation in the beta menu in preferences

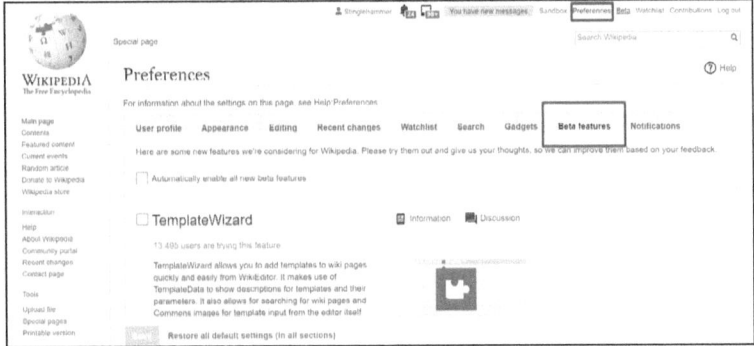

## 3.2. Article selection

There are a number of criteria to be met to ensure the completion of the assignment goes smoothly. The chosen article needs to be:

- one that exists in the source Wikipedia and not in the target language Wikipedia (due diligence is required to check that the article does not already exist under another title);

- 2,000 words or more in length OR multiple articles totalling 2,000 words;

- well-referenced, with inline citations throughout (poorly referenced articles are likely to be deleted if they are published in a new Wikipedia);

- of suitable content and subject matter; and

- reasonably well structured and using language that represents a worthy level of linguistic challenge.

Chapter 6

To this end, students are asked to look first at the featured articles on Wikipedia (the highest quality standard on Wikipedia) and the good articles (the second highest level of quality) to see if any are suitable for translation into another language. These featured and good articles are community reviewed to ensure they are of sufficient quality to appear on Wikipedia's front page (see Figure 3 below).

Figure 3. Featured articles are accessible to view from Wikipedia's front page[4]

The students are also shown how to use other open tools to find potential articles, such as:

- Wikipedia categories, such as 'articles needing translation from foreign-language Wikipedias'[5];

- Wikipedia portals;

- 'Gapfinder' tool[6];

---

4. https://en.wikipedia.org/wiki/Main_Page and https://en.wikipedia.org/wiki/Wikipedia:Featured_articles

5. https://en.wikipedia.org/wiki/Category:Articles_needing_translation_from_foreign-language_Wikipedias

6. http://recommend.wmflabs.org/

- 'Not in the other language' tool[7].

The goal of the Gapfinder tool's developers was to encourage Wikipedia editors to create important articles that are missing in their field of expertise/interest and in the languages they speak. The Gapfinder system (see Figure 4 below) consists of three components:

- finding which articles are missing in the first place by comparing content for every language pair in Wikipedia;

- ranking them by their importance, by predicting pageviews that the article would have, had it existed in the destination language; and

- recommending the most important articles to the best-suited editors.

Figure 4. The Gapfinder tool recommending missing articles from English to Spanish Wikipedia for the search term 'Edgar Allan Poe'

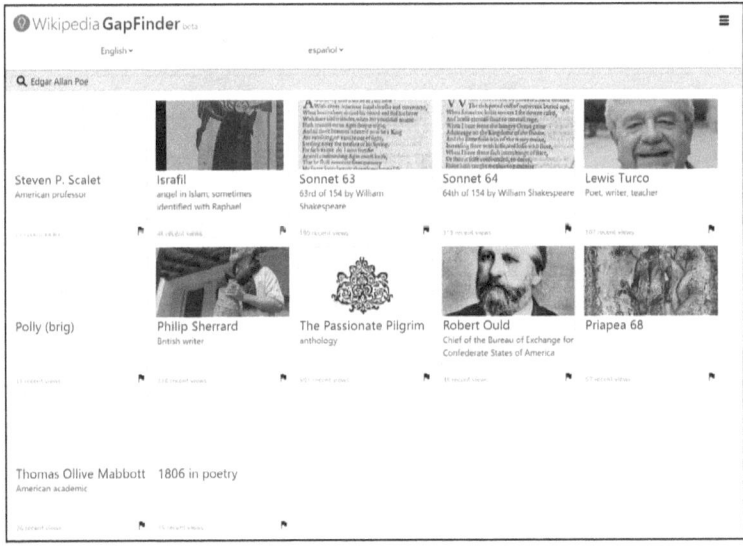

---

7. https://tools.wmflabs.org/not-in-the-other-language/

# Chapter 6

So that no student makes a poor choice of article to translate, they are given advice about how to assess article quality through paying attention to the use of inline citations throughout and the article's rating on Wikipedia's quality scale (stipulated on every article's Talk page). Potential articles are forwarded to the Wikimedian in residence and the teacher who approve them in collaboration, with the teacher assessing the suitability and linguistic complexity of each on a case-by-case basis. Once approval is received from both, then the article link and language pairs are added to the assignment page so the resident, teachers, and other students know which article each student is working on so any confusion (or duplication) is avoided.

The second two-hour workshop – normally held seven to ten days after the first workshop – is when the students get introduced to the Content Translation tool (see Figure 5 below) and begin the process of translating their article. This tool allows editors to create translations right next to the original article and automates the boring steps: copying text across, looking for corresponding links and categories, etc.

Figure 5. The Content Translation tool

The tool does a lot of the formatting work, pulling in text from the source text and automatically providing a machine translation version for most, though currently not all, language pairs, thus allowing students to focus on editing the text to create a translation that will read naturally in the target language. It also warns when the text contains too much machine translation (as shown at 100% in Figure 5 above) as it is Wikipedia consensus that an unedited machine translation is worse than having no article at all. Unedited machine translations are likely to be deleted on publishing. The tool does not have access to the visual editor dropdown menus at present, so students are encouraged to complete all the automated formatting migration, paragraph-by-paragraph, and then publish the resulting article to their personal draft space in the target Wikipedia so that more editing checks can be done ahead of publishing to the live space (see Figure 6 below). The cog wheel icon allows users to publish directly to the live article space in the target language Wikipedia or a draft space so that more editing work can be done there before publishing.

Figure 6.  Publishing from the Content Translation tool

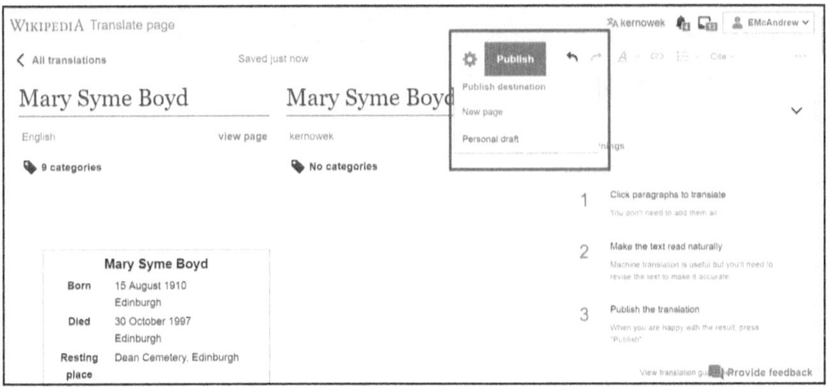

The second workshop provides students with an opportunity to see how to begin translating, check whether machine translation is available for their language pairs, and set up a draft space on the target language Wikipedia for working on the article outside of the Content Translation tool.

Drop-in clinics are offered every two weeks in a computing lab for students to ask the Wikimedian in residence formatting questions, otherwise students are left to work independently on the assignment.

The students are required to publish their translations by the end of the penultimate week of the semester, and to notify the Wikimedian when they are ready to do this, in case there are any issues at the point of publication. The students also upload Microsoft Word documents of their source article and translated article, complete with word count, to the institution's virtual learning environment.

### 3.3. Learning points – developing a successful methodology

To ensure a successful assignment, it is important to have someone who is 'Wikipedia-literate' to support the students and ensure they focus their efforts on *translating* rather than formatting articles. The Wikimedia Foundation has national chapters around the world who can be contacted as a first port-of-call for discussing the Wikimedian in residence model or in order to identify local Wikimedia volunteers who could support such an assignment.

Selecting an appropriate article at the beginning of the assignment is important to ensuring the translation does not run into issues on publishing, e.g. students publishing articles that already exist in the target Wikipedia, that are very similar to other articles, that have been worked on by their classmates, or have unreferenced sections. Following the criteria outlined above and making use of featured articles, good articles, and the Gapfinder tool are recommended to avoid such issues.

Checking the word count of the source article is useful for students to ascertain whether the translation will be an appropriate length for the assignment. While the Search tool can be used to look up articles, it includes references in its word count so it is not accurate enough for the purposes of the assignment. Students are advised instead to copy the main body of the article's text, excluding notes, references, bibliographies etc., into a Word document to determine a more accurate word count. Alternatively, the Word Count tool (see McAndrew, 2017), created by Dr Alex Chow of the University of Edinburgh, can be used to count the words of the main text of any article on English Wikipedia.

Although preparing the assignment in the right way is important, it is also helpful to ensure the article is published in accordance with Wikipedia's norms and conventions, so an 'aftercare' methodology has also been developed. Publishing newly translated articles is an important juncture for anyone supporting translation workshops or assignments. Although the Content Translation tool helps with removing a lot of the headaches associated with formatting new Wikipedia pages, a number of elements may need to be checked over, in particular:

- Does the article contain too much machine translation?

- Does it read naturally?

- Is it well structured and coherent?

- Is it well-referenced? Are there sufficient inline citations throughout the article?

- Are any paragraphs misaligned?

- Has the tool struggled with copying across citations, tables, infoboxes, etc.?

- Have images been copied across correctly? (This includes checking licenses).

- Are there any typos, grammatical errors, or empty headings?

If any of these issues have occurred the article should not be published onto the target Wikipedia until they are corrected.

Once students are logged in to Wikipedia, they can tick the blue star icon on a page to add it to their Watchlist (see Figure 7 below). This means they will be notified of any changes to the articles and can monitor them during the important first few days of their infancy on the target Wikipedia.

Chapter 6

Figure 7. The template boxes added to the Talk page newly created for the new Wikipedia article for the Sami Assembly of 1917[8]

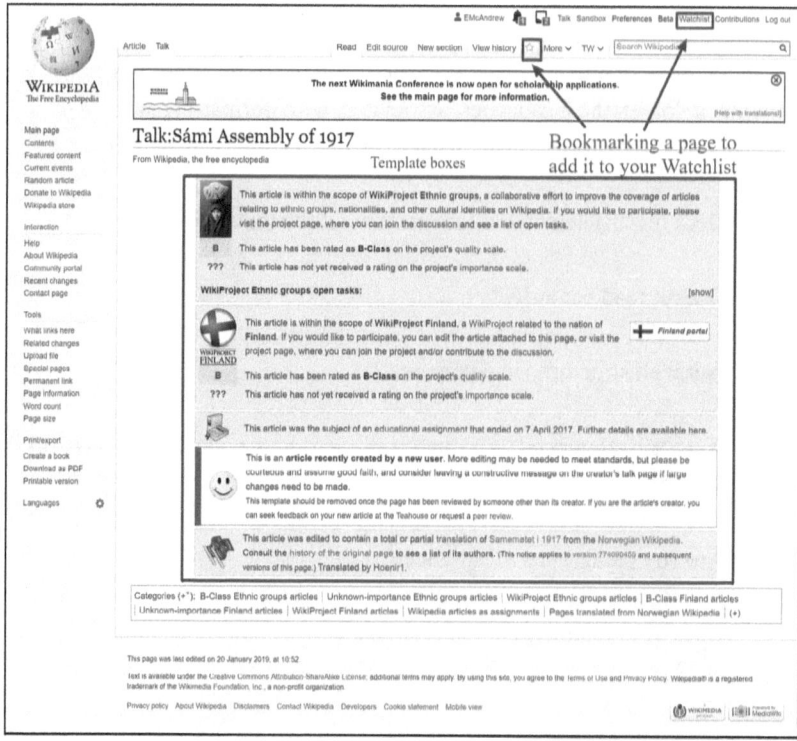

Template boxes can be added to the article to flag up that the student editor is a new user, the article is still being worked on, is a translated page, or is part of an education assignment, etc.

### 3.4. Feedback from students and staff

An online survey was emailed to students at the end of the assignment to complete anonymously. The seven questions consisted of a mix of Likert scale responses and free text answers. This had 19 student responses in 2016/2017:

---

8. https://en.wikipedia.org/wiki/Talk:Sami_assembly_of_1917

- ten out of 19 respondents selected *Very Much So* when asked if their topic was interesting and relevant to their course;

- seven out of 19 respondents selected *Somewhat* when asked if their topic was interesting and relevant to their course; and

- only two respondents of the 19 selected *Not very much* and *Not at all* when asked if their topic was interesting and relevant to their course.

There were ten responses in 2017/2018. The 2017/2018 results included an extra Likert scale question on digital literacy which revealed that:

- seven out of ten agreed with the statement: *I better understand how to evaluate online information*;

- seven out of ten agreed or strongly agreed with the statement: *I better understand how to use and share online information*; and

- six out of ten agreed with the statement: *I have become better at creating and contributing to online information.*

Upon completion of the second semester's Wikipedia translation assignment, video interviews were also conducted with the course leaders and students to elicit feedback on their experience of the assignment (see supplementary materials for more detailed data). Feedback from students indicated that:

- they were engaged and enthusiastic about Wikimedia's mission to share knowledge globally;

- they were selecting texts they were interested in;

- they were getting much-needed published translation practice which they could use when getting a job;

- they were learning new skills and developing information and digital literacy; and

- they were enjoying the assignment.

Participating teachers were pleased that the students were:

- getting the necessary practical experience they needed;

- engaging in problem solving and critical thinking;

- engaging with how knowledge is shared around the world;

- writing neutrally for a Wikipedia audience;

- considering the verifiability of the information they were presented with;

- evaluating to what extent the translator should ever intervene; and

- learning academic research and writing skills which should stand them in good stead for their dissertation.

## 4. Conclusion

Far from being anathema in academia, this case study has demonstrated that Wikipedia has a lot to offer to teaching and learning, particularly in the context of teaching languages and translation. Translating between different language Wikipedias is a really impactful way to help build understanding between language communities and helps students to: (1) understand how knowledge is created, curated, and contested online; (2) create a new open educational resource that lasts beyond the lifetime of their assignment and can be added to and improved as a community project over time; and (3) achieve much-needed and *meaningful* published translation practice ahead of entering the world of work.

## Acknowledgements

We would like to thank the Translation Studies MSc programme directors: Dr Charlotte Bosseaux, Dr Hephzibah Israel, and Dr Şebnem Susam-Saraeva. We would also like to thank the course teachers, our colleagues at information services and the Wikimedians who helped support the project including Melissa Highton, Anne-Marie Scott, Dr Richard Nevell, Leila Zia, and Amir Aharoni among many others. Finally, we would like to record our special thanks to the Translation Studies MSc students without whose industry and enthusiasm for the project none of this would have been possible.

## Supplementary materials

- More detailed evaluation data: https://research-publishing.box.com/s/eid6c0b9ijm4oi3k7ls4f59dzgoqr5lf

- Lesson plan for how to conduct Wikipedia editing training: https://commons.wikimedia.org/wiki/File:How_to_conduct_Wikipedia_Editing_Training_(lesson_plan).pdf

- Sample assignment page for the Wikipedia translation project: https://en.wikipedia.org/wiki/Wikipedia:University_of_Edinburgh/Events_and_Workshops/Translation_Studies_-_2018/2019_Semester_One

- Screencast demonstrating the Content Translation tool: https://upload.wikimedia.org/wikipedia/commons/e/ee/Content_Translation_Screencast_%28English%29.webm

- SPLOT Wikipedia Translation workshop resource: https://thinking.is.ed.ac.uk/wikitranslation/

- Wikimedia UK website and contact details: https://wikimedia.org.uk/wiki/About_us

Chapter 6

# References

Al-Shehari, K. (2017). Collaborative learning: trainee translators tasked to translate Wikipedia entries from English into Arabic. *The Interpreter and Translator Trainer, 11*(4), 357-372. https://doi.org/10.1080/1750399x.2017.1359755

Martínez Carrasco, R. (2018). Using Wikipedia as a classroom tool — a translation experience. *Proceedings of the 4th International Conference on Higher Education Advances (HEAd'18)*. https://doi.org/10.4995/head18.2018.8112

McAndrew, E. (2017, May 10). *Word Count tool - counting the prose text in a Wikipedia article*. [Online Video]. 10 May 2017. https://media.ed.ac.uk/media/1_kfx9b4q5.

Selwyn, N., & Gorard, S. (2016). Students' use of Wikipedia as an academic resource — patterns of use and perceptions of usefulness. *The Internet and Higher Education, 28*, 8-34. https://doi.org/10.1016/j.iheduc.2015.08.004

The University of Edinburgh. (2019a). *Degree finder* [online]. https://www.ed.ac.uk/studying/postgraduate/degrees/index.php?r=site/view&edition=2019&id=251

The University of Edinburgh. (2019b). *Vision and mission.* [online]. https://www.ed.ac.uk/governance-strategic-planning/content-to-be-reused/vision-and-mission

Wales, J. (2016). *Wikimania conference, Esino Lario, Italy.* https://wikimania2016.wikimedia.org/wiki/Main_Page

# 7. Working with online communities: translating TED Talks

## Anna Comas-Quinn[1] and Mara Fuertes Gutiérrez[2]

### Abstract

This project aimed to explore how online open communities and resources could be used for language learning in a higher education context. Advanced language learners were introduced to translation and subtitling, and the use of open content to maintain their language skills post-graduation whilst engaging in a meaningful activity, namely sharing knowledge through translation in a volunteer project. Students were asked to translate the subtitles of a Technology, Entertainment, and Design (TED) or TEDx Talk of their choice and to review and provide feedback on two of their peers' translations. Most students enjoyed the activity, particularly being able to choose the talk they would be translating and having access to other students and volunteers to ask questions and get support with the linguistic and technical aspects of subtitling. A small number of students found the technical aspects of the activity challenging and did not enjoy the unpredictability of working in an open community.

Keywords: open pedagogy, volunteering, translation, subtitling, language learning.

---

1. The Open University, Milton Keynes, England; anna.comas-quinn@open.ac.uk; https://orcid.org/0000-0002-8290-4315

2. The Open University, Milton Keynes, England; mara.fuertes-gutierrez@open.ac.uk; https://orcid.org/0000-0002-9890-5945

How to cite this chapter: Comas-Quinn, A., & Fuertes Gutiérrez, M. (2019). Working with online communities: translating TED Talks. In A. Comas-Quinn, A. Beaven & B. Sawhill (Eds), *New case studies of openness in and beyond the language classroom* (pp. 101-113). Research-publishing.net. https://doi.org/10.14705/rpnet.2019.37.969

Chapter 7

## 1. Context of the project

New learning opportunities have emerged as a result of the possibilities the internet affords to connect with others with similar interests, as well as the proliferation of online tools and resources, many of them openly available. Online communities or affinity groups (Gee, 2005) can be profitably used by language educators and learners in both formal and informal learning contexts to create a learning experience that is more authentic, situated, and experiential (Kiraly, 2016; Risku, 2010) than the traditional learning activities routinely offered to learners in the language classroom. And yet, language teachers are still not making full use of these opportunities, with notable exceptions (Al-Shehari, 2017; Martínez-Carrasco, 2018; Wikipedia Education Program, 2012). In fact, it is often language learners themselves who are proactively and independently engaging with available online language learning opportunities (Rosell-Aguilar, 2016, 2018; Sauro, 2017).

The project described here uses a wide definition of open practice (Beetham, Falconer, McGill, & Littlejohn, 2012; Weller, 2017) rather than narrower definitions that focus strictly on the use of openly licensed content (Wiley, 2017). Open practice is making use of open tools and resources but here it is also about connecting with online communities that operate by taking advantage of these open tools and resources. In essence, it is about changing educational practise to involve language learners and teachers in new ways of learning that benefit from openness and the possibilities of tackling meaningful tasks outside the physical or virtual walls of the classroom.

The project recruited graduates specialising in French, German, or Spanish at The Open University, a distance learning university in the UK, who, having recently completed their studies, were interested in exploring ways of keeping up their language skills beyond formal education. A free six-week online course was provided offering three different activities based on the use of freely available online resources: a collaborative cross-language discussion on the topic of migration in Europe; a taster of Massive Open Online Courses in the foreign language; and an introduction to subtitling TED Talks.

All participants described themselves as confident online learners, which was important given that the pedagogical approach relied heavily on self-direction and independent work and the activities required quite sophisticated digital literacy skills. Participants volunteered to take part in the project and decided which and how many of the activities on offer they would complete, according to their interests and availability. This chapter deals only with the activity on subtitling TED Talks: from the 41 volunteers who signed up to the course, 15 completed the subtitling activity described in this case study.

## 2. Intended outcomes

The overall project used a student-centred approach that extended the supported, personalised open learning strategy already employed at the institution. A key aim was to direct learners to existing resources – in this case open tools and resources used by the TED Translators online community to translate the subtitles of TED Talks – which students could use independently to practise their language skills beyond formal education. Another key focus was to make the learning engaged and meaningful, in the sense that learners could take part in real-life tasks with real-life impacts. For the case presented here, this was achieved by working with TED Translators, an online community of "volunteers who subtitle TED Talks, and enable the inspiring ideas in them to crisscross languages and borders" (TED, n.d.).

Beyond these two overarching aims, the activity allowed learners to develop a wide range of skills, both subject specific, such as translating, subtitling, reviewing, and proofreading; and transversal, including information technology, and digital literacy and participatory skills such as online research, communication, and collaboration.

Personalisation was fundamental and was achieved by allowing students to choose the talk they wanted to translate and which language they wanted to translate from or to (in combination with English, the common language in this context). The advantage of TED Talks is that they are self-contained with content

Chapter 7

that is very up-to-date and covers a vast range of topics. They also provide a multicultural dimension (specially TEDx Talks[3] organised locally across the world) and an opportunity for learners to hear and learn from a wide variety of voices. The TED Talk, though sometimes criticised (Robbins, 2012), is well known for its predictable but engaging format and this, together with choice and the topical nature of the content, makes for an interesting and motivating activity for learners.

## 3.  Nuts and bolts

TED Translators is a community of some 30,000 volunteers who produce subtitles in over 100 languages for TED, TEDx, and TED-Ed[4] Talks. Anyone can join, although volunteers are asked to be fluent in at least two languages and familiar with subtitling best practice.

Figure 1.  The TED Translator online profile

3. https://www.ted.com/participate/organize-a-local-tedx-event/before-you-start/what-is-a-tedx-event

4. https://www.ted.com/watch/ted-ed

104

Two things make TED Translators a useful learning resource: a very well structured workflow, which follows the traditional translate-review-approve system and involves two rounds of feedback from more experienced volunteers; and well developed support resources for volunteers, including online video tutorials, subtitling guidelines, and other translation resources collected in a wiki, and language coordinators, who help other volunteers through the review process and in language-specific Facebook groups.

Another aspect that makes TED Translators attractive for language learners is the online profile that translators set up, which acts as a portfolio where volunteers' published work can be showcased (see Figure 1 above).

### 3.1. Tools and resources

The activity was hosted on an institutional Moodle page with an associated forum where students could access support from their tutors and fellow students.

Figure 2.  The Amara subtitling editor

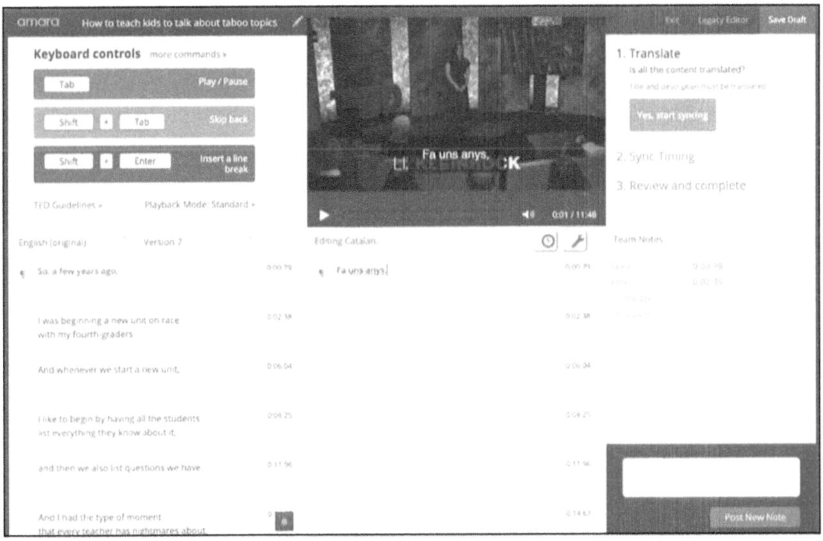

Students needed to register with the TED Translators project and use the open source Amara[5] online subtitling editor to translate their chosen talk (see Figure 2 above). They were also directed to additional support resources (see supplementary materials). Most participants carried out the tasks using their desktop or laptop computers.

### 3.2. Brief description of the activity

Students were asked to translate the subtitles of one short TED or TEDx talk. In the course of six weeks, students learnt about the TED Translators community and resources, the basics of translating and subtitling, and how to use the subtitling editor Amara. They worked from and into the language of their choice in a mixed group (French, German, and Spanish in combination with English), and, with the support of the facilitators and fellow students, they discussed translation problems and choices, and reflected on the linguistic and extra-linguistic challenges posed by the activity. The activity required both independent and collaborative tasks.

In Week 1, students created their profiles in TED and Amara and learnt how to locate resources and access support groups in order to be fully equipped to start their translation. They were advised to choose a video on a topic of their interest no more than ten minutes in duration to ensure that the task was manageable within the allocated time. In addition, they took part in a forum discussion about the main principles of translation and, in particular, about translating for TED Translators.

During Weeks 2 and 3, participants worked on their translations independently, although they had the option of seeking help from both the facilitators and fellow students in the forum, and other volunteers in the TED Translators language-specific Facebook groups. Students were instructed not to submit their completed translation in the Amara platform, instead they were asked to share it through the activity forum to be peer reviewed by fellow learners.

---

5. https://amara.org/en/

Weeks 4 and 5 were devoted to peer reviewing and feeding back on each other's translations. Students were instructed to select two translations to review in their own language combination, giving priority to those that had not been chosen yet. Facilitators stepped in to provide reviews for those translations that had not been reviewed by other learners (as numbers were not even in every language). During this time, facilitators led a discussion in the forum on the differences between reviewing and assessing, how to give constructive feedback, and how to deal with reviewers' comments. This round of peer-review was designed to support students in improving their translation before submitting the final version in the Amara platform to be officially reviewed and approved for publication by other TED Translator volunteers. The inclusion of this preliminary peer-review step was considered essential given the unpredictable timings of the reviewing system in TED Translators. Experience gained through participation in TED Translators and through a previous project using TED Translators with learners in educational contexts (Cámara & Comas-Quinn, 2016) revealed that delays in the reviewing process had a negative impact on participant motivation. All tasks in TED Translators are carried out by volunteers, who chose which talks they translate or review according to their preferences and interests, and this results in some talks awaiting reviews for many months. It was therefore deemed necessary to incorporate a scheduled review step carried out by fellow learners in the design of the activity. Once their work had been reviewed by other learners and students had made the final changes to their translation, they were free to choose whether they wanted to submit their work through Amara for review, approval, and publication. This step was optional as it was considered ethically more appropriate for students to make the decision on whether they wanted to publish their work online (Martínez-Arboleda, 2013).

In Week 6, students prepared and submitted an assignment consisting of a reflection in English (800-900 words) discussing three translation problems, covering linguistic, cultural, and technical aspects they had encountered whilst completing the task.

## 3.3. Evaluation

The evaluation of the project was conducted through a post-course survey for which ethical approval had been secured, consisting of a total of 26 questions combining both closed (particularly multiple-choice and Likert scale questions) and open-ended questions. Although 41 of the 45 participants who joined the course had initially showed interest in this activity, time constraints led to many withdrawals from those who decided to focus on one of the other course activities. Hence the much lower number of students (15) who completed the task and responded to the survey.

The results of the survey reveal that the majority of students were very positive about the activity: all but one indicated they enjoyed 'having choices about which online services and technologies to use' and agreed it was an important element of this activity. In addition, although most of them had never shared their work online – with three of them having done so only through short postings – all of them reported feeling confident about publishing their translations.

The main drawback related to open content was that almost a third of students experienced some difficulties accessing content or resources related to the activity. The most common challenge reported was the complexity of the TED/ Amara registration processes, as well as lack of familiarity with both platforms, which is consistent with the fact that a third encountered some or very much difficulty with technology, particularly with Amara –and just under half did not experience any difficulty at all. Regarding time, nine participants reported spending between two and four hours, and six of them between four and five hours per week working on this activity.

With regards to the learning experience itself, it is interesting to note the mixed results when students were asked to judge the level of difficulty of this activity compared to other language learning they had done at the institution at an advanced level. Half found the activity to be similar in difficulty to other work they'd undertaken in their formal studies, whilst the rest were split between those who found this activity harder and those who found it easier than their previous experiences of language learning. This could perhaps be linked to the previous experiences that each individual student had with translation tasks or, again, with the specific technological challenges that this activity presented. Also related to the learning experience, all respondents, with the exception of one participant who encountered multiple difficulties, concluded that the activity helped them to improve their language skills. Students highlighted that the task helped them to clarify their ideas about translation and subtitling, including finding strategies for dealing with hidden meanings or learning about the importance of researching cultural references. Some participants also mentioned they liked learning about the TED Translation project and about the topic of the talk. Regarding the assignment, all students judged a reflective essay an appropriate assessment instrument. However, many other types of assessment are possible and could be more suitable in other learning contexts, depending on the focus given to the activity (translation quality, collaboration, terminology...).

Another part of the evaluation asked students about the study and transversal skills they had developed whilst working on the activity. All participants responded that 'development of my autonomy as a learner' was an important element of this activity and, with one exception, they declared themselves 'confident in directing their own work', particularly once they became familiar with TED and Amara, despite some of them admitting feeling overwhelmed, nervous, etc. at the beginning of the task. Collaboration, however, was not considered as important as 'developing my autonomy' in the context of this activity. Nonetheless, two thirds of participants selected positive responses to the question on the extent to which the activity had improved 'learning with others rather than individually' – perhaps thanks to the peer-review process they engaged in – and a similar number judged helpful or very helpful the effectiveness of support and guidance from their peers. With regards to research and Information and Communication Technology (ICT) skills, almost all respondents considered that the activity had helped them improve in both areas, although some of them found it more demanding in terms of ICT skills than other activities in their previous studies.

Finally, looking at motivation and enjoyment, the vast majority of students indicated they enjoyed the learning process, with two thirds choosing 'very much' and only one student selecting 'very little'. Amongst the aspects that students enjoyed the most were learning new skills, such as translation, subtitling, and problem-solving, making sure that the quality of the end result was good enough for public viewing and, in connection to this, the fact that the activity had a real-life impact and made a valuable contribution to society. Conversely, a simplification of the technical aspects (TED and Amara) or of the peer-review process (both the internal and the external steps) would have improved their experience.

Facilitators and task designers were also asked to give feedback on their experiences whilst running the project: on the positive side, they mentioned the activity exceeded their expectations with regards to students' collaboration, participation, and engagement, and considered it a success and a model of online collaboration. On the negative side, they expressed concerns about some students' being able to fully direct their own work. Some issues in understanding the facilitator's role were also identified, signalling that more work needs to be done to help facilitators embrace the role of supporting independent learning. With regards to this, it is worth noting that only half of the respondents engaged with the facilitators, but those who did found the support provided very helpful.

## 4. Conclusion

In summary, students enjoyed having choices and tackling a 'real world' task. They felt the activity supported their language development (both in their native and target languages), and the development of applied language skills in translation and subtitling, as well as digital and ICT skills. They also mentioned personal gains, such as enjoyment, the opportunity to find out about TED Translators or finding a new hobby. Meanwhile, facilitators had to deal with the tension between providing support and allowing problem-solving skills to be developed, as some students found the TED and Amara platforms complicated. This project shows that using open tools and resources, and engaging with the communities where these are used, has huge potential for language learning and teaching, both as a way of connecting learners with real world activities that have an impact on society, and as a means of developing their language and applied skills.

## Acknowledgements

We are grateful for the assistance of Lou McGill in the evaluation of the activity described in this case study.

## Supplementary materials

List of resources provided to students:

- TED Translators Guidelines: https://www.ted.com/participate/translate/guidelines

- TED Translators Subtitling resources: https://www.ted.com/participate/translate/subtitling-resources

- TED Translators Wiki OTPedia: https://translations.ted.com/Portal:Main

- TED Translators Main guide: https://translations.ted.com/TED_Translator_Resources:_Main_guide

- TED Translators generic public group in Facebook (in English): https://www.facebook.com/groups/ITranslateTEDTalks/

## References

Al-Shehari, K. (2017). Collaborative learning: trainee translators tasked to translate Wikipedia entries from English into Arabic. *The Interpreter and Translator Trainer, 11*(4), 357-372. https://doi.org/10.1080/1750399x.2017.1359755

Beetham, H., Falconer, I., McGill, L., & Littlejohn, A. (2012). Jisc open practices. Briefing paper. https://oersynth.pbworks.com/w/page/51668352/OpenPracticesBriefing

Cámara, L., & Comas-Quinn, A. (2016). Situated learning in open communities: the TED Open Translation Project. In P. Blessinger & T. J. Bliss (Eds), *Open education: international perspectives in higher education*. Open Book Publishers.

Gee, J. P. (2005). Semiotic social spaces and affinity spaces. From the age of mythology to today's schools. In D. Barton & K. Tusting (Eds), *Beyond communities of practice: language, power and social context*. Cambridge University Press.

Kiraly, D. (Ed.). (2016). *Towards authentic experiential learning in translator education*. Mainz University Press.

Martínez-Arboleda, A. (2013). Discovering Spanish voices abroad in a digital world. In A. Beaven, A. Comas-Quinn & B. Sawhill (Eds), *Case studies of openness in the language classroom* (pp.176-188). Research-publishing.net. https://doi.org/10.14705/rpnet.2013.000119

Martínez-Carrasco, R. (2018). Social media in L2 education: exploring on-line collaborative writing in EFL settings. In F. Rosell-Aguilar, T. Beaven & M. Fuertes-Gutiérrez (Eds), *Innovative language teaching and learning at university: integrating informal learning into formal language education*. Research-publishing.net. https://doi.org/10.14705/rpnet.2018.22.772

Risku, H. (2010). A cognitive scientific view on technical communication and translation. Do embodiment and situatedness really make a difference? *Target, 22*(1), 94-111.

Robbins, M. (2012, September 10). The trouble with TED Talks. *NewStatesman*. https://www.newstatesman.com/martin-robbins/2012/09/trouble-ted-talks

Rosell-Aguilar, F. (2016). User evaluation of language learning mobile applications: a case study with learners of Spanish. In A. Palalas & M. Ally (Eds), *The international handbook of mobile-assisted language learning* (pp. 545-581). China Central Radio & TV University Press.

Rosell-Aguilar, F. (2018). Autonomous language learning through a mobile application: a user evaluation of the busuu app. *Computer Assisted Language Learning, 31*(8), 854-881. https://doi.org/10.1080/09588221.2018.1456465

Sauro, S. (2017). Online fan practices and CALL. *CALICO Journal, 34*(2) 131-146.

TED. (n.d.). *TED Translators*. https://www.ted.com/participate/translate

Weller, M. (2017, April 12). *My definition is this*. http://blog.edtechie.net/oep/my-definition-is-this/

Wikipedia Education Program. (2012). *Case studies: how professors are teaching with Wikipedia*. Wikimedia Foundation. http://upload.wikimedia.org/wikipedia/commons/0/03/Wikipedia_Education_Program_Case_Studies.pdf

Wiley, D. (2017, April 4). *How is open pedagogy different?* https://opencontent.org/blog/archives/4943

# 8. Repurposing MOOCs for self-regulated language learning in an English for academic purposes course

### Barbara Conde Gafaro[1]

## Abstract

This case study investigated the self-regulated learning strategies that university students employ while engaging with Massive Open Online Courses (MOOCs) as part of an English for Academic Purposes (EAP) course. Self-Regulated Learning (SRL) involves the processes whereby students plan, monitor, evaluate, and adjust their performance towards goal attainment. Literature from MOOCs identifies self-regulation as an essential feature of participants who successfully take part in such courses. Learners are anticipated to monitor their learning while working with the online material at their own pace and connecting with other learners around the world whenever they want. Using MOOCs as supplementary learning material for a face-to-face academic English course provides an interesting picture of the learning strategies that students use while embracing openness within a formal learning context. This paper reports on the data collected from two online questionnaires administered to identify and compare the SRL strategies that participants used before and after their MOOC engagement. Semi-structured interviews were also conducted to complement the quantitative data. Data analysis shows that strategic planning and metacognitive monitoring strategies tend to be used more than help-seeking strategies during MOOC engagement. Findings also highlight students' positive attitudes towards the study

---

1. The Open University, Milton Keynes, United Kingdom; blcg2@open.ac.uk

**How to cite this chapter:** Conde Gafaro, B. (2019). Repurposing MOOCs for self-regulated language learning in an English for academic purposes course. In A. Comas-Quinn, A. Beaven & B. Sawhill (Eds), *New case studies of openness in and beyond the language classroom* (pp. 115-128). Research-publishing.net. https://doi.org/10.14705/rpnet.2019.37.970

Chapter 8

as well as their suggestions for future blended MOOC practices within academic English courses.

**Keywords: self-regulated learning, MOOCs, English for academic purposes, SRL strategies, blended learning.**

## 1. Context of the project

Language learning materials for specialised domains tend not to be widely available (Colpaert, 2016). This becomes an obstacle when attempting to present relevant materials to students who come from different areas of study to the EAP classroom. In a previous case study conducted by Beaven (2013), EAP students worked with MOOCs related to their fields of education as a way to compensate for the lack of well-designed subject-specific published materials in English.

MOOCs, which represent the development of online learning at a massive scale (Daniel, 2012), are designed around the presentation of subject-specific resources (Sokolik, 2016). MOOC learners use a variety of strategies (de Waard, 2015; Littlejohn & Milligan, 2015) which are essential to regulate one's learning (Zimmerman, 2000). Therefore, this case study examined the use of MOOCs not only to supplement classroom activity, but also to identify students' self-regulatory strategies in an EAP course offered at the University of Ferrara in Italy.

The EAP course ran for eight weeks, from February to April 2018. During 15 sessions, students had two hours of classroom contact twice a week. Thirteen students from different study programmes took part in the project: five PhD candidates, three Masters students, and five undergraduates. Most of the participants had a B2 level of proficiency in English, which was adequate for engaging with the academic content of the MOOCs, since at this level students can understand the main ideas of complex texts in their academic fields (Council of Europe, 2018).

## 2. Intended outcomes

SRL is conceptualised as a process in which it is proposed that students assume responsibility for their learning through three cyclical phases – *forethought*, *performance*, and *self-reflection* – during which a series of strategies will be carried out to guide, regulate, and inform their learning (Zimmerman, 2000) (Figure 1). In language education, SRL occurs when students deploy metacognitive, cognitive, and social strategies to regulate their learning (Read, Bárcena, & Rodrigo, 2010).

Figure 1. Recent version of SRL cyclical model (adapted from Zimmerman & Moylan, 2009, in Panadero, 2017, p. 5)

**PERFORMANCE PHASE**

*Self-Control*

Task strategies
Self-instruction
Imagery
Time management
Environmental structuring
Help-seeking
Interest enhancement
Self-consequences

*Self-Observation*

Metacognitive monitoring
Self-recording

**FORETHOUGHT PHASE**

*Task Analysis*

Goal setting
Strategic planning

*Self-Motivation Beliefs*

Self-efficacy
Outcome expectancies
Task Interest/value
Goal orientation

**SELF-REFLECTION PHASE**

*Self-Judgment*

Self-evaluation
Causal attribution

*Self-Reaction*

Self-satisfaction/affect
Adaptive/defensive

Similarly, MOOCs tend to provide a flexible learning structure (Beaven et al., 2014) to create spaces for self-regulation. Research on MOOCs has begun to focus on exploring language education (Appel & Pujolà, 2015; Beaven, 2013; de Waard & Demeulenaere, 2017). However, there is little research in the field that examines students' self-regulation when taking MOOCs within their academic language courses.

MOOCs afford opportunities to engage with organised academic content (Margaryan, Bianco, & Littlejohn, 2015) which students can use to practise English (Beaven, 2013; de Waard, 2015). The wide range of courses offered in English – 7,548 courses announced by the time of writing (Shah, 2018) – represent an opportunity for students who seek to improve their EAP while accessing knowledge that may be relevant to their disciplinary specialisms. With this in mind, this study was intended to:

- identify the strategies that EAP students use to regulate their language learning before and after working with MOOCs;

- encourage the connection of their language learning process with their academic area of interest.

## 3.    Nuts and bolts

In Week 1 of the EAP course, all participants from different study programmes (see supplementary materials, Appendix 1) completed an online pre-questionnaire to identify the self-regulation strategies they were aware of using when taking a language course and to explore their previous familiarity with MOOCs. The instruments employed to survey participants' SRL processes were adapted from the Motivated Strategies for Learning Questionnaire (Pintrich, Smith, Garcia, & Mckeachie, 1991) (see supplementary materials, Appendix 2).

From the second to the fifth week of the course, participants chose a MOOC related to their academic field and engaged with the material and activities that they considered useful to their language learning needs. They were asked to use Class Central (https://www.class-central.com/), a search engine tool to browse MOOCs by subjects, providers, and universities. Although participants were free to choose what course content and activities they engaged with and how and when to do so, a minimum of two hours of study per week was advised.

In Week five, 11 out of the 13 participants completed an online post-questionnaire to identify the self-regulation strategies they were using after engaging with the MOOC. Subsequently, voluntary semi-structured interviews were conducted in Weeks 6 and 7 of the course. Four interviewees expanded on the beliefs, opinions, and attitudes they held with regard to their MOOC learning experience by responding to pre-elaborated guiding questions adapted from an interview designed by Littlejohn and Milligan (2015) to probe SRL sub-processes of MOOC users (see supplementary materials, Appendix 3). The findings obtained from both online questionnaires and the semi-structured interviews are discussed below.

At the outset of this study, the familiarity that participants had with MOOCs was limited. None of them had ever completed a free online course before. However, in completing the online pre-questionnaire, participants framed their expectations of doing such online courses under the terms of *variety, flexibility*, and *autonomy*. Based on their initial perspectives, free online courses: (1) cover multiple subjects that fit different people's interests; (2) can be accessed anytime; and (3) do not have fixed schedules, so people can decide when to start or leave the course, select a particular topic, and review it as much as they want. Some of the participants also referred to these courses as a chance to improve their comprehension of spoken discourse related to their research fields (Participant 8); an opportunity to increase vocabulary and discuss with other users (Participant 17); and "a possibility to approach the language in a different and interesting way" (Participant 13).

Zimmerman's (2000) SRL cyclical model was employed during data collection and analysis of the findings. The items of both questionnaires were structured around the three phases and six sub-phases outlined in Zimmerman's (2000)

SRL cycle (Figure 1). In the first questionnaire, participants were asked to rate the set of items related to their typical learning behaviour in a language course. By contrast, the statements in the post-questionnaire focussed on participants' language learning behaviour in the MOOC they chose as part of their EAP course. Based on the data gathered from the pre- and post-questionnaires, it was observed that participants had different reasons to planning their learning before enrolling in both a language course and a MOOC (Figure 2).

Figure 2. Results from the pre- and post-questionnaires about strategic planning

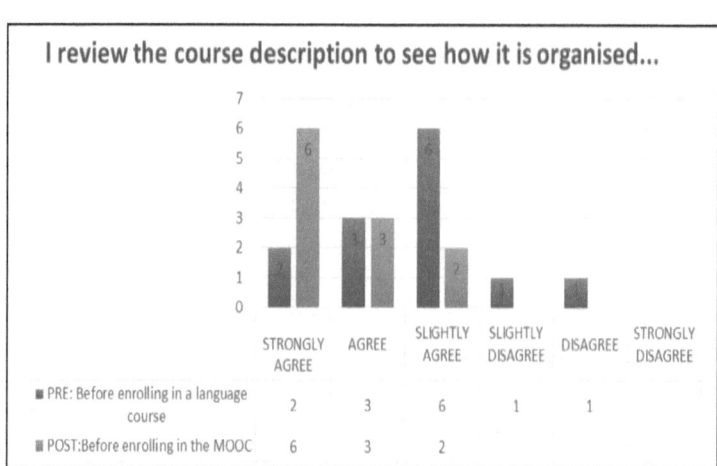

Before enrolling in the language course, participants tended to check the course description, to be prepared for upcoming learning activities. In contrast, before enrolling in the MOOC, participants were more likely to check the course description to see how it was generally organised. One of the respondents, for example, stated: "I had a first look of the material, and I saw ok there are some videos, there are some papers to read, but it's not too much. Ok, yeah I can do it. I found it readable and feasible in general" (Participant 6). This slight difference in strategic planning carried out in the *forethought* phase might be associated with a lack of prior experience of MOOCs on the part of participants, hence the need to have an overview of the structure and topics of the online course they decided to work on during their EAP course.

Choosing a MOOC related to the participants' study programme was useful to compensate for the possible uncertainty that doing a MOOC for the first time involved. Being familiar with the content of the MOOC helped some of them focus more on their language skills, such as understanding the video-lectures, improving vocabulary, and presenting the course material to others in a clear way. Likewise, practising English while studying a relevant subject online allowed students to expand their academic knowledge, as outlined in some of the comments from the interviews:

> "even if my first aim was to improve vocabulary, then I found some interesting topics that could be related to my research field and my doctorate research proposal, so I started to following this MOOC to find, to search for other resources and also courses abroad so, for example, this one was related to a specific institution in Amsterdam related to Urban Planning" (Participant 1).

> "And, the best thing was that we had some links and references where we can study from them" (Participant 15).

Figure 3. Results from the pre- and post-questionnaires about help-seeking strategies

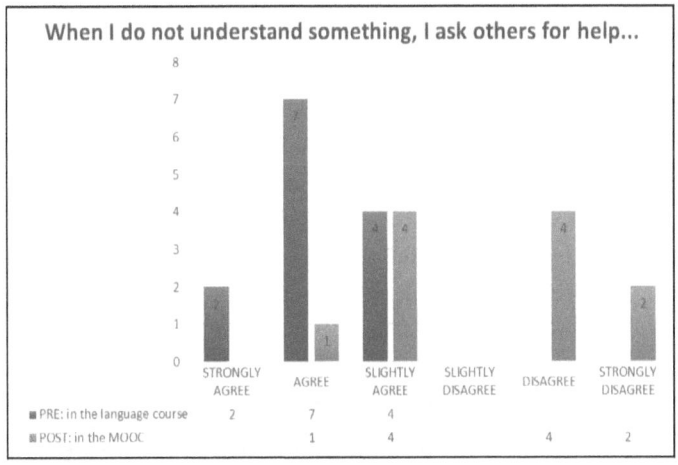

Chapter 8

Figure 4. Results from the pre- and post-questionnaires about task strategies

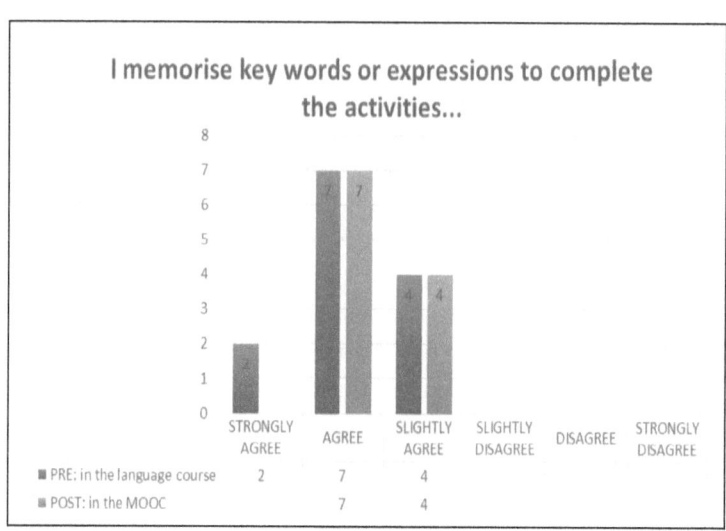

Regarding participants' *performances*, they rarely translated new information from the language course and their MOOC into their native language. Help-seeking strategies were employed less during the MOOC engagement. However, memorisation was a task strategy equally used in both courses, as observed above (Figure 3 and Figure 4).

Metacognitive monitoring strategies, which are part of the self-observation processes (Figure 1), were also identified in the responses to questionnaires and interviews. Informal mental tracking of what participants were studying in the language course and the MOOC was mainly done by note-taking and by asking themselves questions to ensure they understood the course content. These strategies also helped some participants to be more aware of the strengths and weaknesses of their language skills while working with MOOCs, as pointed out by two of the interviewees:

> "It was very useful for my listening because of course, I had to watch the video and try to understand everything, so it's like to watch a TV

series in English, but in this case it was a very good opportunity because it was about what I studied so again it was like I'm back in my Erasmus experience with the English teacher that they talked about Law and the module wasn't so easy because in general Law is not easy, so it was very great for me to improve again" (Participant 15).

"Maybe I never thought about using a MOOC actually to learn English and the course itself gave me the idea to use the MOOC as a way to improve pronunciation, and to be able to speak and compare the speaking with the reading [the video script] because for example, I've been pronouncing the same words all over the years in a completely wrong way but I could not have the perception of it for example by watching a film or a TV series and I found this useful" (Participant 1).

Self-observation processes are often linked to the processes involved in the *self-reflection* phase. Being aware of their learning strategies led some participants to reflect on and adjust the way they were engaging with their MOOCs. One of the interviewees illustrates this point clearly:

"At the beginning, I started like… a university exam. So, I had the idea to do all and to finish it. And then I realised it was not the good strategy for a MOOC then I did, for example, two or three hours a week. And, in that time I did ok, today I am gonna do some writing, today I am gonna do something about reading… so I divided the thing or the MOOC with some little aim week by week. So, that was the process, the work I did with the MOOC" (Participant 5).

Participants not only engaged with the content and activities in the MOOC, but also made decisions on how to best approach the online material based on self-observation and reflection on their initial tactics in working with these online courses. In the last phase of the student's SRL process, self-judgment and self-reaction come together to influence the next round of forethought and performance sub-processes – thus, completing the self-regulating cycle (Zimmerman, 2000). Besides, informal reflection on – and adjustment of – participants' learning

# Chapter 8

behaviours in the MOOC played an important role in determining levels of interest and self-satisfaction when working with MOOCs, and this was observed while coding the four semi-structured interviews (Figure 5).

Figure 5. Main codes obtained from the interviews' transcriptions

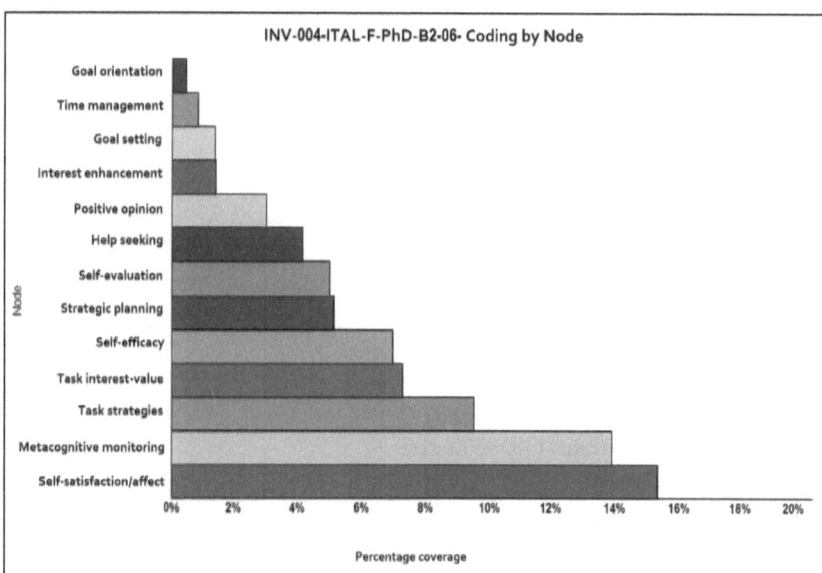

The recorded interviews were transcribed and exported to the software package, NVivo. Then, a deductive approach to the coding of the transcriptions was carried out (Silver & Lewins, 2014), i.e. data was coded and grouped into themes corresponding to the self-regulatory phases and six sub-phases identified in Zimmerman's (2000) SRL cycle. Emerging codes such as positive or neutral opinions were also linked to participants' feedback of the project obtained from the post-questionnaire.

By the end of the study, participants were asked to summarise the experience of doing a MOOC as part of their EAP course. Overwhelmingly, they were pleased with their MOOC selection, describing it as: "a helpful and new experience that was surely useful to fulfil the purposes why I enrolled in the

EAP course" (Participant 4); "very satisfying and challenging" (Participant 9); and "an interesting, and sometimes even funny way of learning something new" (Participant 18). Only one of them expressed discomfort with the MOOC and preferred a face-to-face learning approach by stating: "I think frontal lessons are much more interactive and efficient. I did not like it very much" (Participant 8).

Although MOOCs were not completely integrated into the language classroom, students were asked to give a presentation about the MOOC they chose to their classmates. During the interviews, participants mentioned the use of strategies to help them prepare for this oral activity such as note-taking, drawing diagrams, and selecting specific topics from weeks of the course that were relevant to them. Lastly, participants discussed the merits of choosing MOOCs related to their interests, or different academic fields of theirs, as well as doing more speaking activities for future MOOC practice within academic English courses.

## 4. Conclusions

MOOCs, which have their roots in open educational resources and connectivist pedagogy, tend to be openly available to people around the world regardless of prior qualifications or professional experience. The open nature of such courses has led teachers and researchers to integrate MOOCs into the classroom as a pedagogical practice within the language education field. Nevertheless, there is little research that follows a blended MOOC approach for investigating self-regulatory processes in academic language courses.

This case study of SRL focussed on the level of strategic processes employed by university students who used MOOCs as supplements to an EAP course. Specific self-regulatory strategies employed by participants when engaging with digitally-enabled resources in MOOCs were identified after administering two online questionnaires and conducting semi-structured interviews. Findings show that participants were more likely to employ strategic planning and metacognitive monitoring strategies than help-seeking strategies during MOOC engagement.

In this light, the present case study suggests that working with MOOCs as part of an EAP course provided participants with an alternative learning approach whereby they had access to courses in specific disciplines that fitted their degree programmes as well as their language learning needs. Participants described this study as a new experience that took their language learning beyond the classroom. Accordingly, teachers are encouraged to implement blended MOOC practices within academic language courses. Lastly, it is advised to examine the self-regulatory processes that occur during the inclusion of such open educational courses within particular language classroom activities, thus closing the gap between classroom learning and open learning.

## Acknowledgements

I would like to thank my supervisors from The Open University, Dr Tim Lewis, Dr Tita Beaven, and Dr Rebecca Ferguson, for their support and wise words that have contributed towards my research journey, and a special thank you to Dr Ana Beaven for letting me contact her students to be part of this case study.

## Supplementary materials

https://research-publishing.box.com/s/9j8hwoqjwp497xckj06p049xfpm9n71o

## References

Appel, C., & Pujolà, J. T. (2015). Pedagogical and technological issues in the instructional design of a tandem MOOC. In *Proceedings of E-Learn: World Conference on E-Learning in Corporate, Government, Healthcare, and Higher Education* (pp. 1696-1705). Association for the Advancement of Computing in Education (AACE).

Beaven, A. (2013). Using MOOCs in an academic english course at university level. In A. Beaven, A. Comas-Quinn & B. Sawhill (Eds), *Case studies of openness in the language classroom* (pp. 217-227). Research-publishing.net. https://doi.org/10.14705/rpnet.2013.000122

Beaven, T., Hauck, M., Comas-Quinn, A., Lewis, T., & de los Arcos, B. (2014). MOOCs: striking the right balance between facilitation and self-determination. *Journal of Online Learning and Teaching, 10*(1), 31-43.

Colpaert, J. (2016). Foreword. In E. Martín-Monje, I. Elorza & B. G. Riaza (Eds), *Technology-enhanced language learning for specialized domains: practical applications and mobility* (pp. xvii-xx). Routledge.

Council of Europe. (2018). *Global scale - table 1 (CEFR 3.3): common reference levels*. https://www.coe.int/en/web/common-european-framework-reference-languages/table-1-cefr-3.3-common-reference-levels-global-scale

Daniel, J. (2012). Making sense of MOOCs: musings in a maze of myth, paradox and possibility. *Journal of Interactive Media in Education, 18*, 1-20. https://doi.org/10.5334/2012-18

De Waard, I. (2015). MOOC factors influencing teachers in formal education. *Revista Mexicana de Bachillerato a Distancia, 7*(13).

De Waard, I., & Demeulenaere, K. (2017). The MOOC-CLIL project: using MOOCs to increase language, and social and online learning skills for 5th grade K-12 students. In Q. Kan & S. Bax (Eds), *Beyond the language classroom: researching MOOCs and other innovations* (pp. 29-42). Research-publishing.net. https://doi.org/10.14705/rpnet.2017.mooc2016.669

Littlejohn, A., & Milligan, C. (2015). Designing MOOCs for professional learners: tools and patterns to encourage self-regulated learning. *eLearning Papers, 42*, 38-45.

Margaryan, A., Bianco, M., & Littlejohn, A. (2015). Instructional quality of massive open online courses (MOOCs). *Computers & Education, 80*, 77-83. https://doi.org/10.1016/j.compedu.2014.08.005

Panadero, E. (2017). A Review of Self-regulated Learning: Six Models and Four Directions for Research. *Frontiers in Psychology, 8*, 1-28. https://doi.org/10.3389/fpsyg.2017.00422

Pintrich, P. R., Smith, D. A. F., Garcia, T., & Mckeachie, W. J. (1991). A manual for the use of the motivated strategies for learning questionnaire (MSLQ). *The Regents of The University of Michigan*, (91-B-004). https://files.eric.ed.gov/fulltext/ED338122.pdf

Read, T., Bárcena, E., & Rodrigo, C. (2010). Modelling ubiquity for second language learning. *International Journal of Mobile Learning and Organisation, 4*(2), 130-149. https://doi.org/10.1504/ijmlo.2010.032633

Shah, D. (2018, January 8). By the numbers: MOOCS in 2017 how has the MOOC space grown this year? Get the facts, figures, and pie charts [Web log post]. https://www.class-central.com/report/mooc-stats-2017/

Silver, C., & Lewins, A. (2014). *Using software in qualitative research: a step-by-step guide.* SAGE Publications Ltd. https://doi.org/10.4135/9781473906907

Sokolik, M. (2016). Academic writing in MOOC environments. In E. Martín-Monje, I. Elorza, & B. G. Riaza (Eds), *Technology-enhanced language learning for specialized domains: practical applications and mobility* (pp. 165-176). Routledge.

Zimmerman, B. J. (2000). Attaining self-regulation: a social cognitive perspective. In M. Boekaerts, M. Zeidner & P. Pintrich (Eds), *Handbook of self-regulation* (pp. 13-39). Academic Press. https://doi.org/10.1016/B978-012109890-2/50031-7

Zimmerman, B. J., & Moylan, A. R. (2009). Self-regulation: where metacognition and motivation intersect. In D. J. Hacker, J. Dunlosky & A. C. Graesser (Eds), Handbook of metacognition in education (pp. 299-315). Routledge.

# 9 Assessing language student interaction and engagement via Twitter

## Olivia Kelly[1]

---

### Abstract

Twitter has over 326 million monthly active users with the number of daily users growing every year since 2016 and is increasingly used by students and academics to interact and build online learning communities. For distance language learners, Twitter offers an open, free, and accessible environment for interaction and engagement which is difficult to replicate in Virtual Learning Environment (VLE) forums. VLE forums have the issue of being module and year specific and are often split into small student groups limiting the opportunity for natural interaction between students. This study aims to build on existing research and assesses the levels of student interaction and engagement via Twitter. The research involved the use of a survey of language students at The Open University (OU), UK, and a virtual ethnographic analysis of tweets related to the term 'OU languages'. The survey asked OU language students about their use of Twitter in relation to their studies and their thoughts on its advantages. The analysis of public tweets related to the term OU languages showed that a large number of different users tweet about the topic, which leads to enhanced interaction between students themselves and their teachers. A sentiment analysis of the words used in the tweets also showed that the tweets are consistently positive, which can lead to increased motivation for students. Overall, the analysis showed that students value the use of Twitter by teachers to give out information and offer support as well as the support they offer and receive from each other during their studies.

---

1. The Open University, Milton Keynes, England; o.m.kelly@open.ac.uk; https://orcid.org/0000-0002-1334-6401

**How to cite this chapter:** Kelly, O. (2019). Assessing language student interaction and engagement via Twitter. In A. Comas-Quinn, A. Beaven & B. Sawhill (Eds), *New case studies of openness in and beyond the language classroom* (pp. 129-143). Research-publishing.net. https://doi.org/10.14705/rpnet.2019.37.971

# Chapter 9

**Keywords:** social media, Twitter, virtual ethnography, interaction, support, engagement, learning communities.

## 1. Context of the project

Use of social media is now widespread, with Twitter having 326 million monthly active users (Cooper, 2019), offering students and teachers open online collaboration in a changing socio-educational context. Hashtags allow learners worldwide to communicate their shared interests (examples include #langchat and #mfltwitterati), with enormous benefits to the education community for self-directed learning and empowering lifelong learners. Twitter offers authentic connections and access to the target language, particularly for distance learners, at no financial cost.

As a teacher, I communicate with students and fellow academics via my Twitter account (@OliviaKellyOU) to share course information and retweet interesting articles. I have gradually built up student followers and also become connected with other academics, often outside of my own higher education institution, the OU. The OU is a distance learning university based in the UK. It has the largest number of students in the country and offers a variety of language degrees (The Open University, 2019). Lecturers with the OU mostly work from home where we lack the opportunity to build academic contacts in the same way as campus-based lecturers. Twitter has provided the opportunity to build my own knowledge and contacts and allows home-based teachers and students to offer and receive support (see Figure 1 below). For example, #Twitterchats which involve a series of set questions being discussed via Twitter synchronously usually over a one-hour time slot, have been enlightening and I was privileged to run one via #LALTCHAT in May 2018 on the topic of using social media for academic debate (@UoL_LALT, 2018).

This chapter researches how Twitter promotes learner communication, including how students find Twitter beneficial in their language learning, in an open environment where students are not restricted to particular courses or student groups and can communicate more widely. These findings can be useful to language teachers considering using Twitter in their teaching practice or to develop their use of social media further. It finishes with recommendations on how language teachers can use Twitter effectively as a language learning and community building resource for students.

Figure 1. Examples of supportive tweets

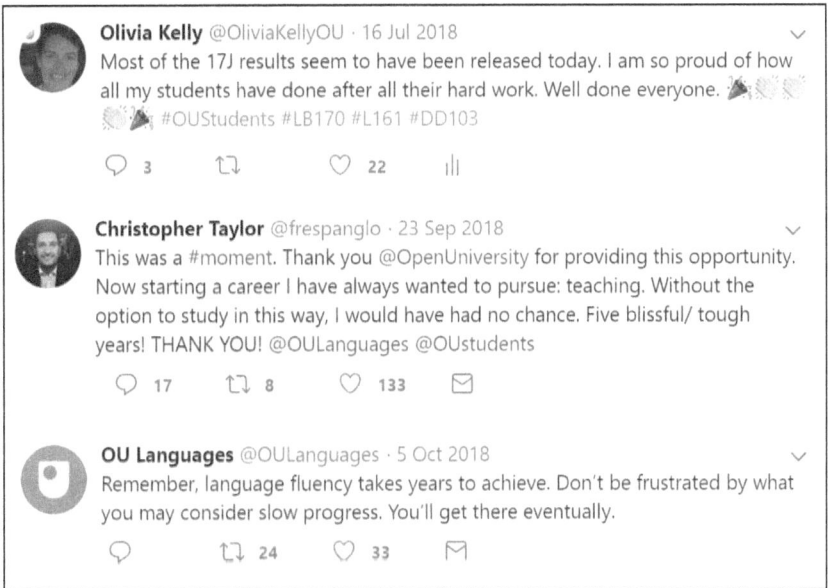

## 2. Intended outcomes

### 2.1. What problems can Twitter solve?

Social media allows distance learning students to interact with each other outside of their own institution's VLE. While chat forums are available, these are split between separate courses and only a few students make regular use of them, perhaps since they require logging in to the institution's site. Social media is now widespread, particularly through mobile devices, allowing students to build relationships in an open environment with more control over their own Personal Learning Network (PLN). Teachers can use open environments in social media to interact with students and highlight suitable news articles, reminders of deadlines, or offer encouragement and support.

### 2.2. Existing research

Some research has already been carried out on how higher education institutions have incorporated social media into their teaching. Hull and Dodd (2017) showed that Twitter was particularly effective in "encouraging contact between students and faculty, promoting active learning, and respecting diverse talents and ways of learning" (p. 98). Hattem and Lomicka (2016) came to similar conclusions in their critical analysis of 17 language learning studies where Twitter was used in a variety of language settings and tasks. They found that Twitter had the potential to promote interaction and communication, and build community. There has been limited evaluation of the impact of this on students, but Ricoy and Feliz (2016) showed student participation increased as students made more use of Twitter and it became "a motivating experience" (p. 237). However, they recognised that this depends on the teachers' "role as dynamisers in the formal incorporation of Twitter in the teaching process, as well as in enhancing interaction between the participants" (Ricoy & Feliz, 2016, p. 237). Most existing research analyses tasks where Twitter participation contributed to assessment, so more research is required to assess how students are using Twitter informally outside of class requirements on a voluntary basis (Rosell-Aguilar, 2018).

### 3. Nuts and bolts

To build on existing research on how students use Twitter for language learning, two types of primary research were carried out. A survey of OU language students active on Twitter assessed if it helps with their learning and contributes towards building a learning community. The @OULanguages Twitter account was set up in 2014 and is run by the languages department. It currently has over 3,600 followers and regularly tweets about language related topics. Using virtual ethnography (a research approach for studying social interactions in virtual environments) to assess how OU language students behave and interact in the digital environment of Twitter, a statistical analysis was carried out on tweets related to the term OU languages.

## 3.1. Tweet analysis

All the tweets over the period of one month from the 13th of September to the 12th of October 2018 which contained the term OU languages or tagged the @OULanguages account were extracted, returning a total of 198 tweets. These were subsequently recorded in Excel (Appendix 1) under the following headings.

Table 1.  Data variables collected relating to tweets

| Date | Twitter handle[2] | Type of tweet | Words used in Tweet | Number of replies | Number of retweets | Number of likes |
|---|---|---|---|---|---|---|
| 13/09 to 12/10 | 67 different Twitter handles | 67 Original 129 replies | For frequency & sentiment analysis | Maximum: 17 Average: 0.69 | Maximum: 24 Average: 0.97 | Maximum: 136 Average: 4.57 |

*3.1.1.  General trends in tweets*

Table 1 above shows the amount of interactions going on between students and academics using the term OU languages in their tweets. Within only one month's time frame, 67 different people were tweeting using this term. This shows the reach of Twitter and how it allows for open communication where anyone who joins the platform can get involved. Of the 198 tweets, 67 were original tweets, but these led on to 129 replies suggesting that Twitter can build conversation and interaction. The words used in the tweets will be analysed further in Sections 3.1.2 and 3.1.3.

---

2. Username unique to each Twitter user.

Chapter 9

While the average numbers of replies and retweets were below one per tweet, the maximum figure shows that certain tweets can lead to a lot of student interaction, with one tweet getting 24 retweets and another tweet leading to 17 replies (see Figure 1). This shows that while some tweets lead to limited interaction, others can resonate with students and really help to enhance their learning and engagement with their course and the institution. The figures for likes are much higher, which is to be expected as 'liking' a tweet is used regularly by users of the platform to show agreement with or support for a tweet. In this case, the average number of likes per tweet reached nearly five with a maximum of 136, an extremely high amount considering the relatively low number of followers of @OULanguages. Overall, these figures support the argument that Twitter can be effective in promoting student interaction and engagement with each other and with teachers and the course team, as well as being open to a wide range of users.

*3.1.2. High frequency words*

All the words used in the 198 tweets were run through a counter to look for high frequency words. Any word which appeared five times or more is listed in Appendix 1 with common small words such as 'a', 'in' or 'it' excluded. Figure 2 below shows most of these words.

From a quick glance at the words shown above, it is clear that they focus on course and study related content. Even focussing only on the words used more than ten times in those 198 tweets shows the overall positive impression given in this social media context (see Table 2 below).

Table 2. Words used more than ten times

| Students | Languages | Thank | French | Will |
|---|---|---|---|---|
| Good | Course | Great | Just | Module |
| Luck | Enjoy | Now | Time | Year |

Certain high frequency words were to be expected such as 'student' or 'language', but the regular use of support words such as 'enjoy', 'luck', and 'thanks' suggests that students and teachers use Twitter not only to provide information but to support each other.

Figure 2. Word cloud (wordclouds.com) showing high frequency words appearing in tweets related to OU languages

3.1.3. *Sentiment analysis*

The high frequency words appeared to have an overall positive sentiment, but in order to test this fully, a sentiment analysis was carried out on the words identified in 3.1.2 to categorise which words were positive, negative, or neutral in sentiment. Each positive word was given a plus one value, negative words a minus one, and neutral words zero. However, when looking at the list of high frequency words which appeared more than five times, none of them could be considered inherently negative (such as 'bad', 'sorry', or 'tough') and therefore none of the high frequency words received a minus one score. By multiplying the score of plus one by the number of times a positive word was used (for example happy is used eight times so 8 x 1 = 8), a score of 311 was achieved (see Table 3 below), which represented the overall sentiment score of the interactions (see Sheet 2 of Appendix 1). This shows that the sentiment of the tweets related to OU languages is overwhelmingly positive in tone and that students and teachers alike use Twitter in a positive way to interact with peers, the course, and their learning.

Table 3. Examples of positive high frequency words and their frequency

| Happy (8) | Love (7) | Congratulations (7) |
|---|---|---|
| Thank/Thanks (25) | Great (12) | Enjoy (10) |
| Overall sentiment score: 311 | | |

Figure 3. Images of encouraging tweets related to OU languages

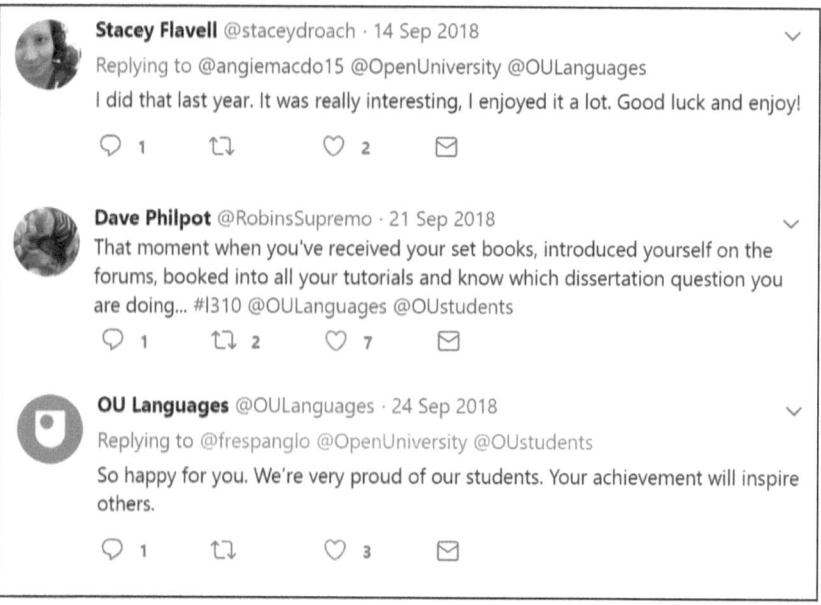

Twitter, and social media in general, has often been regarded as a negative arena where users are open to abusive messages. However, this research has shown that in this particular academic language learning environment within Twitter, this is rarely the case and instead, Twitter, as a platform open to all language learners, offers a positive support network to those users. The mutual respect fostered in class or VLE forum discussions simply migrates to the more open social media platform. Figure 3 above shows examples of how students support each other, and how support and encouragement is offered by teachers.

### 3.1.4. Overall findings

Overall, the evidence shows that students and teachers are creating positive interactions in this open online space. Students appreciate having direct access to those associated with the university in order to receive information related to their studies but also to be able to communicate their enjoyment of the course and celebrate their successes. As a distance learner, the opportunity to interact in this sociable and non-pressurised way is an excellent open resource for students and we as language teachers can assist them in this space in their language learning and engagement with learning. Students can, over time, build their own PLN which they can continue to stay in contact with even when their studies end. This provides the dual purpose of helping students throughout their studies and assisting with retention between courses. Overall, this can lead to greater student interaction and engagement not only within Twitter but in their current course and during their full degree pathway.

## 3.2. Survey research on OU language students using Twitter

A pilot survey was designed to directly ask OU language students how they used Twitter alongside their language study and to assess its benefits to them. A copy of the questionnaire along with response data can be seen in Appendix 2. It attracted only a small number of participants (n=13) but did show interesting results in relation to how students use Twitter as part of their study and, in some cases, their language acquisition.

### 3.2.1. General use

One of the starkest results from the survey was that almost all respondents (12 of the 13) accessed Twitter daily, showing how regularly the platform is used and how easy it is to communicate with students in this way. However, only two thirds of them said that they accessed Twitter more than once a week specifically with the purpose of assisting with their language learning and studies. Yet, despite not logging in to Twitter specifically with this purpose, they are automatically seeing information posted by those they follow on their timeline. If students are following their teachers or the institutional account, they can be targeted with information related to assessment due dates or upcoming lessons even when they are not seeking this out, leading to increased exposure to this important course information. Twitter would not be a suitable replacement for learning content but it can be extremely useful to drip-feed information and support, which surpasses what can be achieved in VLE forums.

### 3.2.2. Study support

All the students who responded follow Twitter accounts run by OU teachers, with more than half of the students following all the accounts relating to the course they are studying, and are therefore exposed to relevant course information in their timelines. As shown in Figure 4 below, everyone considered following these accounts helpful to some extent, with no-one stating that they found it unhelpful. This shows that students feel this is a positive addition to their studies.

However, only two of the students said they regularly communicate with other OU students via Twitter to help with their language practice or to receive study support, with the vast majority saying they rarely or never use Twitter for this purpose. It appears that many students considered their reason for following course-related Twitter feeds is to access information rather than actively aiming to build a learning community with other students. However, this contrasted with responses to the question on whether Twitter helped students to feel part of an online community. In this case, eight responded with slightly and four definitely, with only one student saying it did not help. These figures would indicate that although students are not actively seeking out a support community, this happens naturally over time as they connect with other OU students and interact using Twitter.

Figure 4. Pie chart showing results from survey Question 6

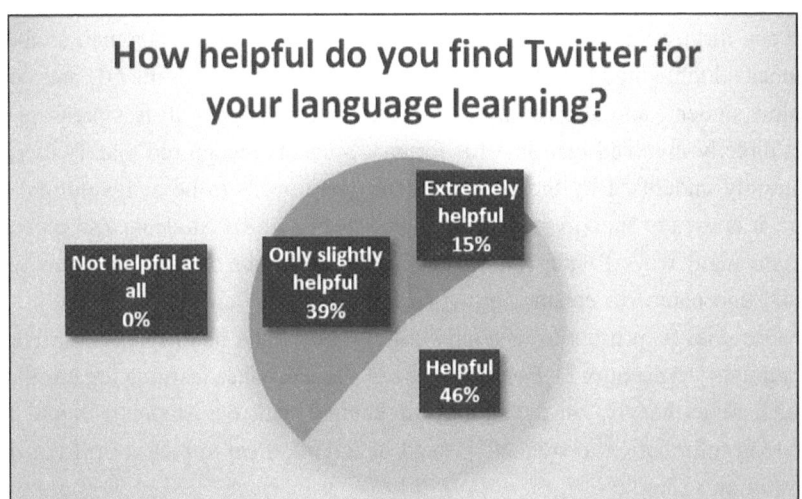

One of the open questions gave students the opportunity to explain how they felt Twitter helped them in their language learning. Responses fell into two distinct categories. Firstly, students identified the ability to view authentic text in the target language as an advantage including news and articles, informal materials, text message language, and colloquialisms. Secondly, while 12 of the 13 respondents found Twitter helped them feel part of a learning community, two students specifically mentioned in the open responses the importance of the support network on Twitter for direct assistance and students sharing best practice tips. One student explains,

> "OU learning can feel that it is a remote experience especially with the cutback on face to face tutorials. Twitter is not a replacement for personal contact but it is a useful tool for sharing experience".

### 3.2.3. Involvement of institution

The final closed question asked if students felt that the OU should be facilitating student communication via Twitter. All the respondents agreed with the OU using Twitter but about half of them felt that support should primarily be offered via the course forums. In the final open question, students were asked for any further comments related to their use of Twitter alongside their studies. Students highlighted that it helped them to communicate with the OU and with fellow students and allowed them to receive information with less pressure to get directly involved than in VLE forums. Students recognised that Twitter is currently underused by the university and there needs to be a 'revolution' in how it is used to support students and give them a voice. Students also pointed out the many ways Twitter can help with communication through use of emojis, links, and photos to enhance a message and that the "character restriction on Twitter does help users to develop skills in precis and identifying/prioritising key points" (Appendix 2). Essentially the OU as a distance learning organisation which relies heavily on technology to interact with our students should be pushing information to students instead of forcing them to pick it up from the institution's sites.

## 4. Conclusions

### 4.1. Top tips

The following tips for language teachers using Twitter have been adapted from Johnson (2009) and Zhang (2018):

- authenticity before marketing – *have personality, inspire conversation;*

- do not just publish news – *personalise for your followers;*

- use separate accounts – *more privacy;*

- reply and retweet – *the more you give, the more you receive;*

- follow everyone who follows you – *it's for conversation and collaboration;*

- take part in chats – *learn from other academics and build your peer community. Try the weekly #LTHEchat, #MFLchat and #AdvanceHE chat*;

- do not tweet about your coffee – *add value to your followers*;

- do not only tweet your own content, participate and retweet – *share news, blogs or tweets from others*;

- do not automate messages – *comes across as spam. If you've time, send a personal message thanking new followers*; and

- limit tweets to five per day – *less is more. Unless taking part in a chat, avoid tweeting lots of messages at once, then being silent for a week. Spread out tweets and keep them relevant.*

### 4.2. What did the research show?

Overall the survey and tweet research has shown that Twitter can offer an open, free, and easily accessible platform for students and teachers to interact and communicate. It helps to build a learning community which supports students and can also support language learning and practice. As Ricoy and Feliz (2016) point out, if universities are to remain innovative, they need to incorporate social media and embrace the digital culture and the opportunities for learning, accessibility, and collaboration that it brings.

## Acknowledgements

I would like to thank Fernando Rosell-Aguilar and the OU languages team for helping to publicise the survey via Twitter, the Student Research Project Panel for their support and advice on the survey, and overall approach to the research and the reviewers for their recommendations. I am especially grateful to the students who took the time to complete the survey and add their views and experience to the research, as well as the students who agreed to have their tweets published in this chapter.

## Supplementary materials

A copy of the data collection materials including the survey questionnaire and Excel data can be found on the IRIS database (https://www.iris-database.org/iris/app/home/detail?id=york:935862): Appendix 1: Excel worksheet containing data on collected tweets and high frequency words and Appendix 2: Survey questionnaire and response data.

## References

Cooper, P. (2019, January 16). *28 Twitter statistics all marketers need to know in 2019.* Hootsuite. https://blog.hootsuite.com/twitter-statistics/

Johnson, B. (2009, August 27). *Twitter… comments on top 10 tips for higher education from DIOSA.* http://bobjohnsonconsulting.com/2009/08/twitter_comments_on_top_10_tips_for_higher_education_from_diosa/

Hattem, D., & Lomicka, L. (2016). What the Tweets say: a critical analysis of Twitter research in language learning from 2009 to 2016. *E-learning and Digital Media 2016, 13*(1-2), 5-23. https://doi.org/10.1177/2042753016672350

Hull, K., & Dodd, J. (2017). Faculty use of Twitter in higher education teaching. *Journal of Applied Research in Higher Education, 9*(1), 91-104. https://doi.org/10.1108/JARHE-05-2015-0038

Ricoy, M. C., & Feliz, T. (2016). Twitter as a learning community in higher education. *Journal of Educational Technology & Society, 19*(1), 237-248. http://www.jstor.org/stable/jeductechsoci.19.1.237

Rosell-Aguilar, F. (2018). Twitter as a formal and informal language learning tool: from potential to evidence. In F. Rosell-Aguilar, T. Beaven & M. Fuertes Gutiérrez (Eds), *Innovative language teaching and learning at university: integrating informal learning into formal language education* (pp. 99-106). Research-publishing.net. https://doi.org/10.14705/rpnet.2018.22.780

The Open University. (2019). *Languages at the Open University*. http://www.open.ac.uk/courses/choose/ppclang

@UoL_LALT. (2018, May 3). *@OliviaKellyOU will be hosting tonight's #LALTCHAT She will be asking the following questions...* Twitter. https://twitter.com/UoL_LALT/status/992035198522060800

Zhang, A. (2018, March 26). *Top five tips that will help you build an online community*. Medium. https://medium.com/@aiaddysonzhang/top-five-tips-that-will-help-you-build-an-online-community-3d0d6581f977

# 10. 'Your language development': harnessing openness to integrate independent language learning into the curriculum

### Tita Beaven[1]

### Abstract

The first module of the online Master of Arts (MA) in Translation at the Open University, Introduction to Translation Theory and Practice, includes a language development strand which encourages students to diagnose their own language development needs and introduces them to tools, resources, strategies, and learning communities that will enable them to independently develop their language skills in both their L1 and their L2, and to consider language development as part of their ongoing professional development as translators, mirroring the practice of many professionals. This chapter consider the extent to which the language development activities and practices can be considered 'open'.

Keywords: translation, lifelong learning, OEP, open pedagogies.

## 1. Context of the project

The Open University (UK) is a distance learning university offering courses in a blended or fully online mode. In 2017, we launched a two-year part-time MA in Translation, which is fully online, partly to mirror the demands of

---

1. The Open University, Milton Keynes, England; tita.beaven@open.ac.uk; https://orcid.org/0000-0002-9074-8789

How to cite this chapter: Beaven, T. (2019). 'Your language development': harnessing openness to integrate independent language learning into the curriculum. In A. Comas-Quinn, A. Beaven & B. Sawhill (Eds), *New case studies of openness in and beyond the language classroom* (pp. 145-156). Research-publishing.net. https://doi.org/10.14705/rpnet.2019.37.972

## Chapter 10

the fast-growing translation services industry. It is delivered on an Open edX platform, enabling students to access the multimedia course content and engage in forum activities related to the course. Students complete three modules (Introduction to Translation Theory and Practice, Translation in Practice, and Extended Translation Project/Dissertation), working to and from English and French, Spanish, German, Italian, Mandarin, or Arabic.

Students are adults, mostly aged between 30 and 60, and 60% female versus 40% male. Most are UK students, although about 40% are from other countries, mainly French, German, Italian, and Spanish. Most have studied languages before, but others come from disciplines including tourism, health, business, or law. As part of the entry requirements for the course, students have to hold a Common European Framework of Reference (CEFR) level C1 in one of their two languages, and a level C2 in the other – equivalent to an International English Language Testing System level seven to eight for one language and above nine for the other.

Students are taught together in each module, completing activities that are offered in the different language combinations and discussing language-specific activities and issues in language-specific online forums. They contribute to more generic discussion in a cohort-wide forum. The tutors, all translation scholars or professionals, provide language-specific feedback on the translation tasks and discussions, give feedback in cohort-wide discussions, and mark and give feedback on their students' assessed work. The first module explores different approaches to translation and the wider cultural, ethical, and professional contexts of translation.

Although as part of the design of the MA we wanted to offer translation activities in all the language combinations to suit the plurilingual nature of the student cohort, we were also aware that, because of time, resources, and the sheer complexity of the instructional design, we would not be able to provide advanced language instruction to the students in all seven languages. In this chapter, I explain how we designed the language development strand of the course using a wide range of open and freely available resources.

## 2. Intended outcomes

It might be argued that students doing an MA in Translation should already possess the advanced language skills necessary to operate between the two languages they are specialising in. Although we require students to have a level C1 in one of their two languages and a level C2 in the other, we also want them to audit their language skills in both their languages, and to evaluate what language aspects (lexical, phonological, syntactical, sociolinguistic, or pragmatic) they need to develop further (Council of Europe, 2001, p. 13). We tell students that, as future translators, they need to constantly update their language skills in both their languages, and we present a number of interviews with professional translators who discuss their approaches to the continuous professional development of their language skills. We also give students the opportunity to explore tools, resources, strategies, and communities to develop their language skills.

## 3. Nuts and bolts

### 3.1. The language development activities

The language development strand consists of the following sections:

- introduction, language proficiency (Week 1): an introduction to the CEFR levels, where students have to assess and record their language proficiency using the Language Passport document on the Europass;

- language proficiency and translator competence (Week 2): an exploration of how linguistic competence fits into different models of translation competence. An analysis of case studies of translation students' language development needs;

- effective language learning habits (Week 3): an analysis of the habits of effective language learners and a personal language development plan for the next four weeks;

- bilingual dictionaries (Weeks 4-5);
- expanding your vocabulary (Week 6-7);
- reviewing your language learning routine (Weeks 8-9);
- monolingual dictionaries and reference books (Weeks 10-11);
- revising your written work (Weeks 12-13);
- language for technical, non-specialised translation (Weeks 14-15);
- developing your research and writing skills (Weeks 18-21); and
- developing your speaking skills (Weeks 22-24).

In the first two sections of their language development work, students look at a number of case studies, select one of them, and write up a short analysis discussing the potential language difficulties this person may encounter as a student of translation, and what their language development should focus on. They share and discuss their analysis in the forum, and then write a short paragraph analysing their own potential language difficulties based on the audit they carry out of their own language competence. They include both their language passport and the analysis of their potential difficulties as a formative section of their first assignment.

### 3.2. Sample case study: Silvia

Silvia is originally from Italy, although she has lived in Scotland for over 30 years. She still speaks Italian with her family and friends back home, and often spends her holidays in Italy, but does not do much else to keep up her Italian. She has occasionally helped in her husband's company, translating emails and invoices, and interpreting when Italian clients have visited. She never studied English formally, and although she speaks it fluently, she is not very confident when writing (see Table 1).

Table 1. Extract from L801: introduction to translation theory and practice

| Mother tongue(s) | Italian | | | | |
|---|---|---|---|---|---|
| Other language(s) | UNDERSTANDING | | SPEAKING | | WRITING |
| | Listening | Reading | Spoken interaction | Spoken production | |
| English | C1 | B2 | C1 | C1 | B2 |

In the third section of the language development strand, students are introduced the habits of highly effective, experienced language learners and consider the practices of these learners in order to formulate a language development plan for themselves. The advice students look at relates to the recent explosion of online language learning resources and language learners' communities on social media based around the polyglot movement. They are introduced to the advice that polyglots provide through their blogs or other social media, and are asked to note the most common tips and techniques and those that they think would be useful to them personally as developing translators.

The advice they look at includes the following blog posts:

- The 7 Habits of Highly Effective Language Learners[2];

- How Polyglots Learn Languages and Stay Sane: Gems of Wisdom from 10 of the Best[3]; and

- How to learn a new language: 7 secrets from TED Translators[4].

The advice provided in these resources suggests that effective language learners:

- have clear goals, and keep the goal in sight;

---

2. https://blog.thelinguist.com/habits-effective-language-learners

3. https://www.fluentu.com/blog/how-polyglots-learn-language/

4. https://blog.ted.com/how-to-learn-a-new-language-7-secrets-from-ted-translators/

- do not cram, but are consistent and work regularly and in short, manageable periods of time to avoid burn-out;

- are not afraid to make mistakes;

- surround themselves with the language and opportunities to use it; and

- make themselves accountable for their own learning.

Students write a language development plan for themselves for the next four weeks, indicating their goals, the main pieces of advice they are going to follow from the expert language learners above, the activities they are going to undertake, and how regularly they will do them, being as specific as possible (e.g. 30 minutes a day/five days a week). They submit their plan as a formative part of their first assignment.

Approximately a month later, students are asked to review their language learning routine and draw up some SMART[5] (specific, measurable, ambitious, realistic, time-bound) goals for their language learning. Again, they are directed to several online resources about goal setting and how to do this specifically for language learning, and they produce a new language development plan for the subsequent six to eight weeks, which they share with fellow-students in the forum and also include as a formative part of their next assignment. Sharing their learning plan and goals with others makes students publicly accountable for the work they have set for themselves, and that public accountability means they are more likely to actually fulfil their plan. Their teacher's feedback also serves to validate their plan, and to motivate them to stick to it.

In later units, we look at specific resources and tools which may be considered more or less 'open'. For instance, the bilingual dictionaries section looks at the online dictionary WordReference[6]. Whereas neither the dictionary data nor

---

5. https://www.mindtools.com/pages/article/smart-goals.htm

6. http://www.wordreference.com/licensing/

the software are openly licenced, the dictionary includes very active language-specific forums where anyone can ask for advice regarding the meaning of specific terms or their translations. Regular contributors are rewarded by being designated as 'Senior members'. In the unit about developing their speaking skills, students read an interview with a practising translator who provides advice about why developing your speaking skills can also be useful in terms of contacting clients in their L1, for instance. Students are introduced to the concept of language exchanges and are encouraged to find themselves a conversation partner. One of the platforms we suggest is italki[7], a language teacher marketplace that also offers language exchange partnerships for free, and that has a strong learning community aspect, where teachers and learners regularly exchange tips, resources, and experiences.

Finally, in the section on language for technical, non-specialised translation, students are introduced to TED talks as a source of language from different technical, non-specialised domains. TED videos cover a wide range of topics including science and technology, business, and global issues in more than 100 languages. TED Translators is a community of volunteers who subtitle TED talks, and in other sections of the course we encourage students to engage with volunteering translation through TED or other online translation communities. Similarly, in the next module, we also include a section on Audio Visual (AV) translation, and encourage students to gain AV technical translation skills through engaging with TED Translators amongst others. However, in the language development strand of the course, we engage with TED talks for the purposes of developing students' technical, non-specialised vocabulary.

In the first activity in this section, students are asked to watch a TED talk: Ramesh Raskar Imaging at a trillion frames per second[8], which explains how femto-photography, a new type of very detailed imaging that visualises objects at one trillion frames per second, works, and its possible future applications. Students are asked to make a list of the terms they would find difficult to translate. As

---

7. https://www.italki.com/partners

8. https://www.ted.com/talks/ramesh_raskar_a_camera_that_takes_one_trillion_frames_per_second?language=en

Chapter 10

with other activities in the language development strand, the discussion includes a 'worked example', where I, as the author of the materials and teacher, explain my own process in dealing with the question:

> "Some of the vocabulary in the list is made up of specialist terms used in this technical area which I am not familiar with. Others, such as 'health/scientific imaging', or the verb 'to open source' are terms that are in my English vocabulary, but I am not sure how to say in my other language. Others, such as 'bullet' or 'pulse' are terms that I understand and can translate, but I am not entirely sure if they have a specialist meaning in this context".

Then, students are asked to find how to translate those terms by using some of the resources previously introduced in the course, such as the forum discussions in online dictionary sites such as Wordreference[9], or the Reverso Context[10] website, which enables users to look up words or expressions and see examples of those words in context and their translations. Finally, they look at the subtitles in their other language to see how these items have been translated.

After this specific activity, students are encouraged to continue using TED talks to find videos that are relevant to the fields they might want to specialise in and build their vocabulary in those areas. Topics range from astronomy to bioethics, health care, microfinance, or urban planning, to name but a few, so students can find relevant material to fit their own interests.

The use of 'worked examples' occurs regularly in the language development strand. For instance, in an activity about using monolingual dictionaries and other reference materials, we consider an extract from *Treasure Island*, a children's classic which students have already looked at in a section of the course on translation and children's literature. The extract, from Chapter 13, reads:

---

9. http://www.wordreference.com/

10. http://context.reverso.net/

"The HISPANIOLA was rolling scuppers under in the ocean swell. The booms were tearing at the blocks, the rudder was banging to and fro, and the whole ship creaking, groaning, and jumping like a manufactory. I had to cling tight to the backstay, and the world turned giddily before my eyes, for though I was a good enough sailor when there was way on, this standing still and being rolled about like a bottle was a thing I never learned to stand without a qualm or so, above all in the morning, on an empty stomach" (Stevenson, 1883, pp. 120-121).

*Treasure Island* contains many references to nautical terms in the various passages about the Hispaniola, the schooner on which the protagonists travel to the island, and a translator might not necessarily be an expert in that terminology. In the activity, students have to look up those terms, and suggest translations into their other language. Throughout the activity, as the teacher and author, I explain how I went about looking these terms up in various resources, and the doubts I had about the meaning or translation of some of those terms. For instance, after looking up the word 'block' in the Oxford Spanish Dictionary, I commented in the course materials: "[m]y intuition tells me that none of those definitions in the dictionary are the right meaning of the word 'block' in the text. To find out more, I would need to look it up in a monolingual dictionary, or in a reference book such as an encyclopaedia. I would also need to look up the word 'boom' to understand what it means in this context", and then I proceeded to look up the terms in other reference materials and to ascertain their meaning in this context. That way, students can understand the process that a translator or experienced language learner might go through when looking up terminology they are not familiar with, and it also serves to reinforce the idea that expert translators, and not just novices, also engage in this type of activity.

### 3.3. But is it open?

The previous section provided an overview of the types of activities and resources that are included in the language development strand of the MA module on Translation Theory and Practice. Some of the activities rely on freely available resources, others on resources that are free AND openly licenced, and others on sites that include communities of users. All these are, to some extent, 'open', but it might be useful to analyse in more detail what this means.

In a recent blog post, David Wiley (2018a), quoting an article by Michael Feldstein (2013), explains how we can conceive courseware as the combination of (1) content, (2) platform, and (3) design. For Wiley (2018a), the content and the platform can be open; open content is content that is openly licenced, and an open platform is one that uses open software. Wiley (2018a) makes the point that often, although the content is open, the platform is not. In the case of the MA module discussed in this chapter, the situation is even more complex in that the platform on which the course is built, Open edX, is open, but the course sits behind a hefty paywall, in the sense that it is only available to students registered on the MA at the Open University. The content is not openly licenced, and the copyright belongs to the Open University. It uses some freely available, online resources that are not openly licenced, and others, such as the TED talks, that are. Wiley (2018b) has coined the term "OER[11] enabled pedagogies" to describe "the set of teaching and learning practices only possible or practical when you have permission to engage in the 5R activities" (n.p.) (i.e. retain, reuse, revise, remix, and redistribute). In that sense, the course cannot be said to adhere to OER enabled pedagogies.

However, in a recent article, Cronin and MacLaren (2018) provide an overview of the Open Educational Practice (OEP) literature and remind us that conceptualisations of OEP vary enormously. Indeed, in an early definition from the Open Educational Quality Initiative (OPAL) project, OEP was defined as "a collaborative practice in which resources are shared by making them openly available, and pedagogical practices are employed which rely on social interaction, knowledge creation, peer learning, and shared learning practices" (Ehlers, 2013, p. 94) with the aim of improving education and promoting innovation. Also in the OPAL project, Andrade et al. (2011) defined OEP as "practices which support the (re)use and production of OER through institutional policies, promote innovative pedagogical models, and respect and

---

11. Open Educational Resource

empower learners as co-producers on their lifelong learning path" (p. 12). In the UKOER project, McGill et al. (2013) suggested that OEP have the potential to "flatten the traditional hierarchy and change the balance of power in learner/ teacher relationships" (p. 10), ideas that have been further developed through the concepts of open pedagogy and open digital pedagogy, with their focus on dialogue, on bringing disparate learning spaces together, and on questioning the power relations that exist within and outside higher education (Cronin & MacLaren, 2018).

The activities in the language development strand of the MA in Translation aim to achieve some of these objectives. Indeed, they rely on interaction between students, on peer learning, and on the sharing of learning practices both within the community of students and beyond, by tapping into the online polyglot community and into communities of learners beyond the university in language exchange platforms. They also emphasise the role learners play in co-producing their own lifelong language learning path, as that is, indeed, the main aim of the language development strand. Finally, through presenting the experience of the author/teacher as a translator in some of the 'worked examples' in the activities, as well as through the interviews with other practising translators about their own lifelong language development work, the course goes some way to flatten the teacher/student hierarchy.

## 4. Conclusions

The language development strand of the MA in Translation course on Translation Theory and Practice aims to enable students to identify their own language learning needs and provide them with the tools, resources, strategies, and communities that will enable them to continue developing their language skills for their rest of their career.

The extent to which the course is open clearly depends on the definition of 'open' that we decide to use. Whilst it is not an OER nor does it fulfil the requirements of an OER enabled pedagogy, I would argue that it conforms to some of the

OEPs identified by the OPAL team and associated with the concepts of open pedagogy and open digital pedagogy. What it also illustrates is the difficulty of applying a seeming 'simple' term such as 'open' to a substantial piece of courseware such as this.

## References

Andrade, A., Ehlers, U.-D., Caine, A., Carneiro, R., Conole, G., Kairamo, A.-K., ... & Holmberg, C. (2011). *Beyond OER: shifting focus to open educational practices*. Open Education Quality Initiative. https://oerknowledgecloud.org/sites/oerknowledgecloud.org/files/OPAL2011.pdf

Council of Europe. (2001). *Common European framework of reference for languages: learning, teaching, assessment*. Language Policy Unit, Council of Europe. https://rm.coe.int/1680459f97

Cronin, C., & MacLaren, I. (2018). Conceptualising OEP: a review of theoretical and empirical literature in open educational practices. *Open Praxis, 10*(2), 127-143. https://doi.org/10.5944/openpraxis.10.2.825

Ehlers, U.-D. (2013). *Open learning cultures: a guide to quality, evaluation, and assessment for future learning*. Springer

Feldstein, M. (2013, April 12). MOOCs, courseware, and the course as an artifact. *e-Literate*. https://mfeldstein.com/moocs-courseware-and-the-course-as-an-artifact/

McGill, L., Falconer, I., Dempster, J. A., Littlejohn, A., & Beetham, H. (2013). *Journeys to open educational practice: UKOER/SCORE review final report*. Jisc. http://bit.ly/HEFCEoerReview

Stevenson, R. L. (1883). *Treasure island*. Roberts Brothers.

Wiley, D. (2018a, February 21). *How do we talk about "open" in the context of courseware?* [Blog post]. https://opencontent.org/blog/archives/5440

Wiley, D. (2018b, May 2). *OER-enabled pedagogy* [Blog post]. https://opencontent.org/blog/archives/5009

# Section 3.

# Openness and teacher development

# 11. Open practices as a catalyst for language teachers' professional development

## Patricia Daniels[1]

### Abstract

This small-scale pilot study enquired into the Open Educational Practices (OEPs) that freelance English language teachers in Switzerland are engaging in and the role these played in their Continuing Professional Development (CPD). Participants are members of a teaching association and work in adult education. Freelancers are often faced with precarious working conditions which can impact on CPD opportunities. Research has shown that engaging in OEP can open up meaningful learning opportunities *in situ*. However, these projects have mainly been in higher education settings where support and training has been offered. Hence, this study explored what freelancers are doing in their natural settings. This project focussed on activities associated with open teaching practices and digital networking practices. Findings are very limited but suggest that open practices can act as an enabler for learning opportunities that lead to knowledge development and improved digital literacy and literacy skills and language skills.

**Keywords**: professional development, open educational resources, open educational practices, freelance English language teachers.

---

1. The Open University, Milton Keynes, England; patricia.daniels@open.ac.uk

**How to cite this chapter:** Daniels, P. (2019). Open practices as a catalyst for language teachers' professional development. In A. Comas-Quinn, A. Beaven & B. Sawhill (Eds), *New case studies of openness in and beyond the language classroom* (pp. 159-171). Research-publishing.net. https://doi.org/10.14705/rpnet.2019.37.973

Chapter 11

## 1. Context of the project

This pilot study is part of an ongoing doctoral research project. It investigated the role that OEP plays in the CPD of freelance English language teachers in Switzerland. Participants are members of a specific teaching association and mainly work in adult education.

The association's primary focus is to promote CPD to keep language teachers in diverse educational sectors up to date with the current English language teaching landscape (see Table 1). Networking and sharing of resources through open platforms and social media channels such as Facebook and Twitter are encouraged. Freelancers are defined here as hourly-paid teachers whose employment is dependent on demand (i.e. student numbers).

Table 1.   Summary CPD opportunities

| Format | Frequency |
| --- | --- |
| **Face-to-Face** | |
| National Conference | 1 x year (2 days) |
| Professional Development Day | 1 x year |
| Regional activities, e.g. workshops, informal meetings | Varies (12 Regions) |
| Special Interest Group (SIG) activities, e.g. informal meetings | Varies (12 SIGs) |
| Reflective Practice Groups | Varies |
| **Content-based/Digital and Print** | |
| Library (Print only) | Always accessible |
| eNewsletter | Monthly |
| Journal (peer-reviewed) | 3 x year |
| Website (diverse resources) | Always accessible |
| SIG eNewsletters | Varies |
| Social media: Twitter, Facebook, YouTube | Always accessible |

Freelancers quite commonly combine hourly contracts or uncontracted work with independent teaching. Consequently, fluctuating employment conditions can impact on wages, CPD opportunities, and motivation. They often work alone, which can lead to a sense of isolation and disconnection from peers. These identified tensions seem to align with those experienced by hourly-paid language teachers in Europe (Beaven et al., 2010; Borthwick & Gallagher-Brett, 2014; Stickler & Emke, 2015).

It is common for freelancers to cater to the needs of different levels of language learners and diverse content areas at any one time. This entails personalising lessons to suit students' needs by creating or adapting resources, digital or non-digital, to supplement or replace coursebook materials which can be costly and time-consuming, particularly where teachers are responsible for supplying resources. Integrating Open Educational Resources (OERs) into their teaching practices and taking part in OEP could mitigate these issues as well as offer students benefits in terms of engagement with more authentic and relevant resources.

Conceptualisations of OEP vary with some being OER focussed and others being more expansive (Cronin & MacLaren, 2018) to include practices such as using open technologies and open teaching practices. This study drew on the Cape Town Open Education Declaration, which views OERs and the open practices associated with them as a vital component of open education, but "also draws upon open technologies that facilitate collaborative, flexible learning and the open sharing of teaching practices that empower educators to benefit from the best ideas of their colleagues" (CTOED, 2018, para.4).

Open technologies such as YouTube, Flickr, and social media tools can facilitate the location, curation, and sharing of OERs (Comas-Quinn & Borthwick, 2015). The affordances of social media tools enable accessible networking where teaching practices and ideas can be shared (Wesely, 2013), personal learning networks can develop (Veletsianos, 2013), and OERs can be discovered or mediated (Hegarty, 2015). This is particularly relevant to freelancers who find themselves working in isolation as this can hinder opportunities to share expertise and peer learning.

## 2. Intended outcomes

Engaging in practices with openly licensed content such as OERs can be challenging. It requires awareness and conceptual knowledge of OERs and licensing frameworks such as Creative Commons (CC) licences[2], as well as understanding the potential benefits of OEP and the value for the individual. CC licences enable users to engage in activities as outlined in Wiley's (2014) 5R framework (retain, reuse, revise, remix, and redistribute). However, the type of CC licence employed can restrict some of these permissions and impact on how resources can be used and shared. Furthermore, sourcing and adapting OERs and using them effectively and confidently in teaching contexts can be problematic when digital literacy skills are inadequate. This is further compounded when access to meaningful CPD that addresses these needs is lacking.

CPD plays a significant role in the learning and development of teachers throughout their careers and is in some research strands inextricably linked to the learning outcomes of students. In contrast to mainstream education in Switzerland, there is no overarching CPD policy for freelancers. Hence, accountability often lies with the individual and is dependent on factors such as self-motivation, agency, personal changing needs, and a willingness to develop professionally (Kyndt, Gijbels, Grosemans, & Donche, 2016). This can be facilitated in part by joining teaching associations, networking, and by learning through tasks embedded in, or connected to, daily teaching activities (Littlejohn & Hood, 2017) whereby bottom-up approaches to CPD are foregrounded.

Top-down approaches to CPD are often critiqued for being unsustainable, inauthentic, unrelated to practice, and do not align with teachers' needs (Opfer & Pedder, 2011; Patton, Parker, & Tannehill, 2015; Webster-Wright, 2009). Consequently, there has been a call for research that focusses on learning opportunities that arise from everyday practices (Evans, 2018; Webster-Wright, 2009). Thus, understanding what freelancers are doing and why in relation to OEPs, and the impact on CPD, can assist the association in supporting them in activities that are embedded into their teaching contexts and consequently, aid in furthering their development in a meaningful way.

---

2. https://creativecommons.org/share-your-work/

Some small-scale qualitative studies involving language teachers (Borthwick & Gallagher-Brett, 2014; Comas-Quinn & Fitzgerald, 2013) have highlighted that there are potential benefits in terms of skills and knowledge development to be gained from engaging with OERs and practices associated with the creation, use, and sharing of these resources.

Hence, this study aimed to capture the value of OEPs in terms of knowledge and skills development from the perspective of freelancers in their natural settings. It explicitly sought to explore and understand:

- types of open practices that freelancers are currently taking part in, if any;

- motives underpinning these practices; and

- whether taking part in these practices is perceived as an enabler for meaningful learning opportunities.

## 3. Nuts and bolts

### 3.1. Research design and methodology

Briefly, data was gathered for this qualitative case study via an online survey and professional conversations (Danielson, 2016). The survey was piloted on the association's National Council (NC) members (n=35) for two reasons, i.e. to test its feasibility for the main study and to avoid imposing on the membership, who will be invited to participate in the main project (2018/2019).

The questionnaire was designed so that interview participants could be identified based on sampling criteria, i.e. being a freelancer, and participation in open teaching practices and/or digital networking practices. The anticipated low survey response rate (22%, eight responded from 35 NC members) limited the survey's use in terms of analysis, but served its purpose as a means of recruiting interviewees.

Three respondents who volunteered for an interview and fitted the selection criteria were interviewed via Skype. The interviews lasted 30 to 45 minutes, were audio-recorded, and transcribed verbatim. The audio-quality of one interview was poor and hence, a follow-up e-interview (Bampton & Cowton, 2002) was utilised to validate the transcription.

Braun and Clarke's (2006) six-phase thematic analysis model was implemented for data analysis and followed a recursive process as illustrated in Figure 1.

Figure 1. Visualisation: phases of thematic analysis (based on Braun & Clarke, 2006)

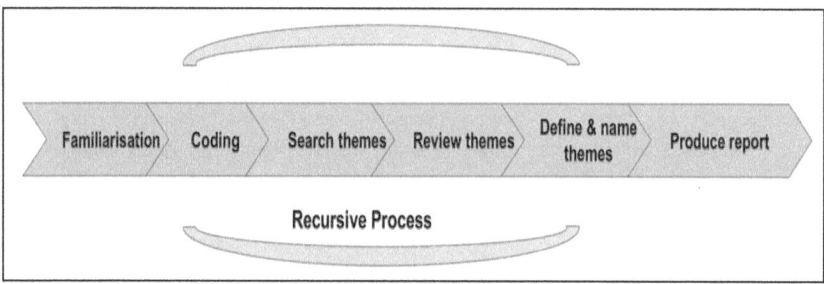

### 3.2. Interview findings

Interview findings are based on data generated from two females and one male and as such are very limited (see summary Table 2). They are experienced teachers and well qualified for their role. Due to the participants being recruited from the NC, further demographics cannot be reported as anonymity has been guaranteed and it could make them identifiable. Participants are referred to as F1, F2 (female) and F3 (male).

Briefly, participants use diverse digital resources such as images, lesson plans, videos with transcripts, and comprehension tasks, but are unaware of CC licences and the term OER, despite their nuanced practices revealing that public domain and openly licensed resources are being used, in part, in their teaching contexts. They source resources through platforms such as One Stop English, BusinessEnglishSite.com, YouTube, and Pixabay. Hence, they use a mix of educational and non-educational sites with little or no attention given to copyright restrictions or default licences. Resources are used to replace or complement course material and are shared by email, social media, or published on participants' blogs. Non-digital resources are shared in face-to-face situations.

Table 2. Summary of findings

| Open Practices | Motivation | CPD |
|---|---|---|
| Teaching practices<br><br>• use of digital resources with and without CC licenses<br>• use of open platforms | Students' needs<br><br>• provide authentic and engaging resources<br>• gain ideas and inspiration<br><br>Professional Development<br>• stay up to date<br>• personal learning<br><br>Professional reasons<br>• self-promotion | Improved:<br><br>• knowledge (content, pedagogical, general)<br>• digital literacy skills<br>• language skills<br>• literacy skills |
| Digital networking practices | Students' needs<br><br>• source authentic and engaging resources<br>• gain ideas and inspiration<br><br>Professional reasons<br>• alleviate isolation<br>• personal learning<br>• self-promotion | |

Students' needs underpinned the motivation for searching, evaluating, and integrating digital resources into lessons. These activities were inhibited where course material is prescribed for the teacher, e.g. F1 commented in relation to using digital resources, "I was teaching at [name removed] and there they had a very specific plan and so then I followed that. There... I'm not as flexible".

The need to provide students with authentic and engaging resources was a motive for adapting digital resources. F1 commented, "students seem to be much more engaged because I can get authentic texts". Adapting resources was perceived as a catalyst to promote critical reflection, e.g. "I think about my students more when you're adapting it rather than just taking a lesson and using it" (F2). Remaining fresh was also a motivational factor, i.e. "I really feel the need to be fresh for everyone, to try something completely different" (F1). This interviewee was fearful of falling behind, i.e. "I think if I don't do it I fear I become obsolete myself" (F1).

Regarding digital networking practices, F1 and F2 use Twitter to network with teachers, search for teaching content, ask questions related to teaching, and for self-promotion. F3 mainly uses LinkedIn to search for articles and resources for his students or for his own development. He connects with other teachers through the messaging system and contributes posts but feels he lacks the skills to use social media effectively for teaching purposes. F1 commented that she blogs "to connect with other teachers" because she sometimes feels lonely as a freelancer.

Concerning the impact of these practices on their CPD, some perceptions overlapped. Regarding digital literacy skills, F3 commented that, "my technical skills have really improved", and F1, "it keeps me up to date... keeps me developing. And I don't ever want to get to the point where I keep using the same old material over and over or just stay stagnant". F3, whose first language is German, perceived an improvement in his digital literacy skills and English language skills by learning how to use PowerPoint so that he could share public domain images in class. He explained that he used the English instructions which are "not necessarily the same as in German. Sometimes, I don't know all the words. You have to read a lot of things, explanations to help yourself. And I learn a lot of new terms" (F3).

Similarly, F2 felt her writing skills had improved through blogging as this involved crafting several drafts and reflecting critically before publishing. F3 commented that "I learn by doing" when asked about how he learns through these practices. F1 linked these activities to lifelong learning particularly when choosing resources for students as this improves her broader general knowledge, i.e. "that's why I do them because I want to keep learning".

All three participants commented that practices such as evaluating and adapting digital resources prompted them to reflect critically on their students' needs and appropriate methodologies. F3 wrote in the e-interview that, "each time I use a resource and adapt it or develop extra materials I feel that I learn something about how my students learn the language. It's the link between my reading and what happens in the classroom".

## 3.3. Discussion

Overall, there seems to be a general lack of conceptual and theoretical awareness of OERs and CC licences which concurs with related research (Falconer, McGill, Littlejohn, & Boursinou, 2013; Masterman & Wild, 2011). However, this does not act as a barrier to reusing or modifying resources, but does seem to limit what resources are being shared and where, which can constrain the potential for peer learning and reuse as they are not being shared openly with a broader audience.

Some of the practices discussed are not necessarily considered 'open' due to the lack of an open licensing framework but, nevertheless, are taking place in online social spaces. Practices associated with social media and participatory tools are enacted in nuanced ways. Sometimes participants engage actively, e.g. take part in open discussions or post comments on blogs and other times participation is peripheral, e.g. follow discussions. In some cases, the latter is linked to limited digital literacy skills and knowledge of how to use specific tools effectively. F3 commented for example, when asked about social media practices, "I don't think that I use them properly".

Initial findings indicate that motivations for taking part in these practices are primarily professional and closely related to students' needs. Evaluation criteria for choosing digital resources included the level of authenticity and the potential to engage and motivate students. In some instances, teachers did not use complementary material due to the prescriptive structure of their courses, which impeded on their autonomy and motivation to make changes in their practices. In these instances, workplace culture seemed to inhibit their agency and limited their engagement in OEP.

Concerning CPD, tentative findings suggest that there is potential for educators to improve their pedagogical, content, and general knowledge, as well as digital literacy and literacy skills and language skills. Additionally, the process of locating, evaluating, and modifying resources for students prompted reflective practice. This is significant in relation to CPD because it can stimulate teachers to think critically about their practices, which can lead to changes in teaching practices, improvements in the quality of teaching (Farrell, 2015; Richards & Farrell, 2005), and perhaps positively impact student learning.

## 4. Conclusion

This study differs from similar small-scale qualitative projects (Borthwick & Gallagher-Brett, 2014; Comas-Quinn & Fitzgerald, 2013) in that it provides insight into what freelancers are doing in real-world contexts. As stated, preliminary findings are very limited. Nevertheless, they indicate that engaging in these practices is contributing in nuanced ways to participants' CPD in terms of skills development, knowledge building, and language literacy. This seems to be occurring through individual and social practices.

Overall, barriers and challenges to engaging in open practices stem from a lack of understanding and awareness of OERs and OEPs and in some cases inadequate digital literacy skills and workplace culture. The latter seemed to restrict the individual's autonomy, agency, and motivation, whereby a lack of digital literacy skills hindered experimentation with specific online tools.

**Looking forward...**

From the association's perspective, findings seem to point to providing support in relation to theoretical and conceptual knowledge of OER and OEP and facilitating the development of freelancers' digital literacy skills.

Concerning the main research project, the survey has been adapted to explore awareness and use of OERs and freelancers' conceptualisations of learning and development that is enabled through participation in OEPs. The interview schedule has been broadened to explore whether improved learning and development through OEPs is leading to changes in freelancers' teaching practices.

## References

Bampton, R., & Cowton, C. J. (2002). The e-interview. *Forum: Qualitative Social Research Sozialforschung, 3*(2), 1-10. https://doi.org/10.17169/FQS-3.2.848

Beaven, T., Emke, M., Ernest, P., Germain-Rutherford, A., Hampel, R., Hopkins, J., & Stickler, U. (2010). Needs and challenges for online language teachers – The ECML project DOTS. *Teaching English with Technology, 10*(2), 5-20. http://cejsh.icm.edu.pl/cejsh/element/bwmeta1.element.desklight-af8eac16-3db6-4969-a70c-4e9e191c08a0/c/1.pdf

Borthwick, K., & Gallagher-Brett, A. (2014). "Inspiration, ideas, encouragement": teacher development and improved use of technology in language teaching through open educational practice. *Computer Assisted Language Learning, 27*(2), 163-183. https://doi.org/10.1080/09588221.2013.818560

Braun, V., & Clarke, V. (2006). Using thematic analysis in psychology. *Qualitative Research in Psychology, 3*(2), 77-101. https://doi.org/10.1191/1478088706qp063oa

Comas-Quinn, A., & Borthwick, K. (2015). Open educational resources for language teachers. In R. Hampel & U. Stickler (Eds), *Developing online language teaching* (pp. 96-112). Palgrave Macmillan. https://doi.org/10.1057/9781137412263_7

Comas-Quinn, A., & Fitzgerald, A. (2013). Open educational resources in language teaching and learning. Higher Education Academy (HEA), Yor (pp. 1-13). http://oro.open.ac.uk/37550/2/874A675B.pdf

Cronin, C., & MacLaren, I. (2018). Conceptualising OEP: a review of theoretical and empirical literature in open educational practices. *Open Praxis, 10*(2), 127-143. https://doi.org/10.5944/OPENPRAXIS.10.2.825

CTOED. (2018). *The Cape Town open education declaration.* http://www.capetowndeclaration.org/read-the-declaration

Danielson, C. (2016). *Talk about teaching! Leading professional conversations* (2nd ed.). Corwin.

Evans, L. (2018). Implicit and informal professional development: what it 'looks like', how it occurs, and why we need to research it. *Professional Development in Education*, 1-14. https://doi.org/10.1080/19415257.2018.1441172

Falconer, I., McGill, L., Littlejohn, A., & Boursinou, E. (2013). *Overview and analysis of practices with open educational resources in adult education in Europe.* JRC Scientific and Policy Reports. https://doi.org/10.2791/34193

Farrell, T. S. C. (2015). *Promoting teacher reflection in second language education.* Routledge.

Hegarty, B. (2015). Attributes of open pedagogy: a model for using open educational resources. *Educational Technology*, (July-August), 3-13. https://doi.org/10.1016/j.calphad.2007.10.001

Kyndt, E., Gijbels, D., Grosemans, I., & Donche, V. (2016). Teachers everyday professional development: mapping informal learning activities, antecedents, and learning outcomes. *Review of Educational Research, 86*(4), 1111-1150. https://doi.org/10.3102/0034654315627864

Littlejohn, A., & Hood, N. (2017). How educators build knowledge and expand their practice: the case of open education resources. *British Journal of Educational Technology, 48*(2), 499-510. https://doi.org/10.1111/bjet.12438

Masterman, L., & Wild, J. (2011). *JISC open educational resources programme: phase 2 OER IMPACT STUDY.* https://www.webarchive.org.uk/wayback/archive/20140614114910/http://www.jisc.ac.uk/media/documents/programmes/elearning/oer/JISCOERImpactStudyResearchReportv1-0.pdf

Opfer, V. D., & Pedder, D. (2011). Conceptualizing teacher professional learning. *Review of Educational Research, 81*(3), 376–407. https://doi.org/10.3102/0034654311413609

Patton, K., Parker, M., & Tannehill, D. (2015). Helping teachers help themselves: professional development that makes a difference. *NASSP Bulletin, 99*(1), 26-42. https://doi.org/10.1177/0192636515576040

Richards, J. L., & Farrell, T. S. (2005). *Professional development for language teachers: strategies for teacher learning*. Cambridge University Press. https://doi.org/10.1017/CBO9780511667237

Stickler, U., & Emke, M. (2015). Part-time and freelance language teachers and their ICT training needs. In R. Hampel & S. Ursula (Eds), *Developing online language teaching* (pp. 28-44). Palgrave Macmillan. https://doi.org/10.1057/9781137412263_3

Veletsianos, G. (2013). Open practices and identity: evidence from researchers and educators' social media participation. *British Journal of Educational Technology, 44*(4), 639-651. https://doi.org/10.1111/bjet.12052

Webster-Wright, A. (2009). Reframing professional development through understanding authentic professional learning. *Review of Educational Research, 79*(2), 702-739. https://doi.org/10.3102/0034654308330970

Wesely, P. M. (2013). Investigating the community of practice of world language educators on Twitter. *Journal of Teacher Education, 64*(4), 305-318. https://doi.org/10.1177/0022487113489032

Wiley, D. (2014). *The access compromise and the 5th R*. https://opencontent.org/blog/archives/3221

# 12. Empowering teachers and learners in and beyond classrooms: focus on OEPs in reading activities

### Fanny Meunier[1], Alice Meurice[2], and Julie Van de Vyver[3]

## Abstract

The present contribution is situated in the framework of a broad government project (entitled Pacte pour un Enseignement d'Excellence) and is specifically devoted to the learning and teaching of modern languages. Our group has been working on the collection, selection, and validation of innovative tools for foreign language learning targeting all levels of proficiency in compulsory education. The present paper reports on a case study that addresses reading strategies outside the classroom for Dutch as a foreign language at A1 level and using a mobile hunt in the Hergé Museum[4] (Louvain-la-Neuve, Belgium). The intended outcomes of our case study include (1) the promotion of mobile and classroom Open Educational Practices (OEPs) for L2 reading, (2) the development of in-service teachers' and learners' digital literacy skills (including among others the co-construction of Open Educational Resources (OERs) and reflective practices on image rights), and (3) the creation of Professional Learning Communities (PLCs) and communities of practice. The Actionbound mobile app was used for the mobile hunt. The participants involved in

---

1. Université catholique de Louvain (UCLouvain), Louvain-la-Neuve, Belgium; fanny.meunier@uclouvain.be; https://orcid.org/0000-0003-2186-2163

2. Université catholique de Louvain (UCLouvain), Louvain-la-Neuve, Belgium; alice.meurice@uclouvain.be; https://orcid.org/0000-0001-7892-1422

3. Université catholique de Louvain (UCLouvain), Louvain-la-Neuve, Belgium; julie.vandevyver@uclouvain.be; https://orcid.org/0000-0001-8820-8340

4. See http://www.museeherge.com/en

**How to cite this chapter:** Meunier, F., Meurice, A., & Van de Vyver, J. (2019). Empowering teachers and learners in and beyond classrooms: focus on OEPs in reading activities. In A. Comas-Quinn, A. Beaven & B. Sawhill (Eds), *New case studies of openness in and beyond the language classroom* (pp. 173-186). Research-publishing.net. https://doi.org/10.14705/rpnet.2019.37.974

Chapter 12

the case study include three researchers, one teacher trainer, 11 pre-service Teachers (psTs) and two classroom groups of Dutch learners (fifth year of primary school). The study setup (including both the teacher training aspects and the activities) is detailed and illustrated, together with the suggestions that emerged from the questionnaires and follow-up focus group discussions.

**Keywords: teacher training, professional learning communities, technology integration, open educational practices, communities of practice, language learning.**

## 1. Context of the project

Our work is part of a government project (in the French-speaking part of Belgium) focusing on quality education and entitled Pacte pour un Enseignement d'Excellence[5]. Within that project, a number of disciplinary consortia have been created. Their aim is to collect, select, test *in situ*, and validate innovative tools for foreign language learning, targeting all levels of proficiency in compulsory education. The present paper reports on a case study carried out in the framework of our involvement in the modern languages consortium which includes researchers and teacher trainers from universities and higher education institutes. The focus of the study is on the practice of L2 reading strategies outside the classroom for Dutch as a foreign language and using a mobile hunt organized in the Hergé Museum in Louvain-la-Neuve.

The participants involved in the case study include three researchers, one teacher trainer, 11 psTs, and two classroom groups of Dutch learners (fifth year of primary school). The data collected in the project relate to two potential target populations: future teachers and young language learners. The study reported here focuses on the first target population, viz. future teachers, and addresses issues related to the use of Information and Communication Technology (ICT) tools by teachers.

---

5. See http://www.pactedexcellence.be/

## 2. Intended outcomes

OERs have been promoted by the EU and UNESCO (n.d.) since the early 2000s. As mentioned by Meurice, Van de Vyver, Meunier, and Delforge (2018), OERs enable international collaboration, facilitate knowledge sharing and policy dialogue between institutions and states (Sabadie et al., 2014), and stimulate learners' interest, satisfaction, and confidence in a task (Bliss, Robinson, Hilton, & Wiley, 2013). However, despite their interest in the potential of OERs, educators to date still have little awareness or knowledge of such resources (Pérez-Paredes, Ordoñana Guillamón, & Aguado Jiménez, 2018). In addition, a lack of digital literacy and media training has been found in pre- and in-service teacher training in French-speaking Belgium (Meurice, 2018), including a lack of sufficient knowledge in copyright licensing (Mishra et al., 2016; Rolfe, 2012).

As the Digital Competence framework for citizens considers copyright and licensing as part of a 'digital creation' competence (Carretero, Vuorikari, & Punie, 2017), our initial aims for the group of psTs involved in the case study were threefold:

- promoting the use of mobile OEPs for L2 reading;

- fostering the development of pre- and in-service teachers' and learners' digital literacy skills, including among others the co-construction of OERs and reflective practices on image rights; and

- creating a local professional learning community and community of practice.

For this experiment, the researchers on the team provided techno-pedagogical support (Lebrun, Lison, & Batier, 2016) to future language teachers (primary and lower secondary school levels) during the creation of a mobile hunt aiming to train L2 learners on reading strategies in the Hergé Museum. The focus on reading strategies and the choice of topics to cover for the game were selected in accordance with one of the official curricular documents, namely the Référentiel

## Chapter 12

de langues modernes – Socles de compétences, 2017[6]. The hunt was created for fifth graders in primary school education who are studying Dutch as a foreign language. It was created in two different versions: a traditional paper version and a mobile one created thanks to the Actionbound[7] application. Actionbound can be considered as an OER as it is a freely downloadable app that can be used by teachers to create digitally interactive scavenger hunts (also called 'bounds'). The specific hunt/bound created for the Hergé Museum is also an OER as it can be reused by other teachers and/or learners.

The overall study setup is summarized in Figure 1 below. After an introduction to the project and its various dimensions (see Section 3), two versions of a hunt were co-constructed by the psTs, their teacher trainer, and the research team. There was a paper version (for the control group of pupils) and a mobile one (for the test group of pupils). The psTs filled in a questionnaire at the end of the activity (to collect their opinions on the activity and on the use of digital technology) and also took part in follow-up focus group discussions.

Figure 1. Overall setup of the project

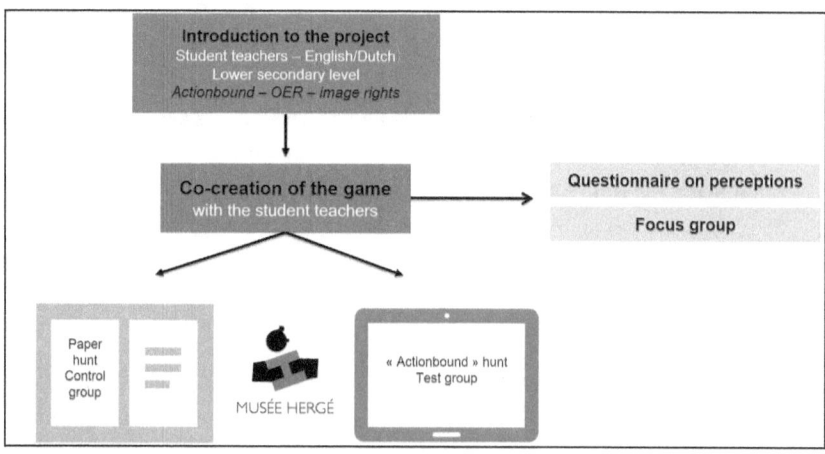

6. The document is available (in French only) online at http://www.enseignement.be/index.php?page=24737&navi=295

7. See https://en.actionbound.com

## 3. Nuts and bolts

During the first encounter with the psTs, one of the researchers introduced the project, together with some theoretical frameworks such as the Substitution, Augmentation, Modification, and Redefinition (SAMR) model (Puentedura, 2013), which presents four different degrees of classroom technology integration (from the lowest to the highest level). Concrete illustrations of pedagogical and technological integration in the language classroom were presented for each level. The various types of licenses and image rights, as well as the different types of OERs, were also discussed (see document link in the supplementary materials section) and the Actionbound app[8] and its features were presented. The app was then concretely tested by the psTs in a practical discovery session via a short hunt that the researchers had prepared. The game was then followed by a visit of the eight rooms of the museum during which the psTs had to identify the reading elements that could be used for the game to be created for the pupils.

In a follow-up session with their teacher trainer, the psTs were divided into groups of two or three, each responsible for two rooms in the museum. They then created questions based on different reading strategies that had been covered in class. To enable effective collaboration and document sharing between the psTs and the researchers, a Google Drive folder was created and the collaboration continued beyond face-to-face meetings via the online platform. Techno-pedagogical support was provided to the psTs to finalize the creation of the game synchronously and asynchronously via the drive. The two versions of the game (see Section 2) were then pre-tested by peers and colleagues and validated by the director of the Hergé Museum with specific attention paid to image rights.

The game, called *Objectif Hergé* (in reference to Hergé's comicstrip *Objectif Lune* [*Explorers on the Moon*]), had to meet different criteria and had to focus on reading strategies. As the pupils' proficiency level (A1) would not allow them to analyze difficult texts and/or rely on complex lexical or grammatical knowledge, the reading strategies practiced had to help them find basic and

---

8. See https://en.actionbound.com/

relevant information autonomously, anticipating, relying on textual and visual elements present in the museum's rooms (i.e. short descriptive texts (available in French, Dutch, and English), pictures, objects, etc.).

The guidelines were provided partly in the learners' mother tongue, i.e. French (see Figure 2 and Figure 3 for illustration). The questions in the game tackled the following themes which correspond to curricular requirements: personal characteristics (name, age, address, telephone, close family, clothing, pets, etc.), daily life, school (understanding classroom instructions, school materials, transportation), home, relations with others (greetings, thanks), and food and beverages (meals and tastes). The game was built for a one-hour visit to the museum and the activity was designed to be 'self-contained' i.e. be doable without prior introduction and easily reusable as an OER by any Dutch teacher and learner. In addition, the game had to respect strict copyright rules. Some features from the app were therefore not exploited to ensure more sustainability (viz. QR codes and geolocation). The two versions of the game (paper and mobile) had to target the same strategies and use the same information within the museum.

Figure 2. Welcome screen of the Actionbound game

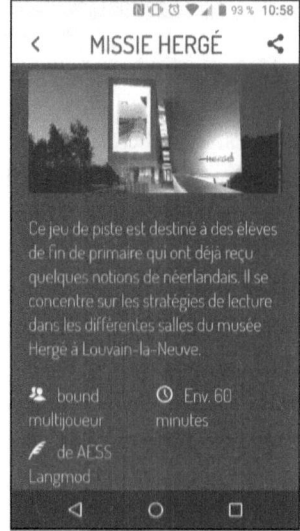

The game consisted in 29 questions in the paper version and 35 in the mobile version (for technical reasons) but the content of the questions was similar. The format of the answers however differed given the functionalities of the Actionbound app (pupils could take pictures, record, or film themselves to answer some of the questions). Gaming elements are also integrated into the mobile app (winning points according to the 'missions' performed and the answers given) and feedback was provided to the pupils after having answered a multiple-choice question for example. Figure 2, Figure 3, and Figure 4 are screenshots from the Actionbound game (or 'bound' as such games are typically called). The complete version is available on the following link: https://en.actionbound.com/bound/objectifherge.

Figure 3.　Sample question – video recording

Figure 4. Illustrations of the gaming options (winning points during the mission) and of the feedback provided

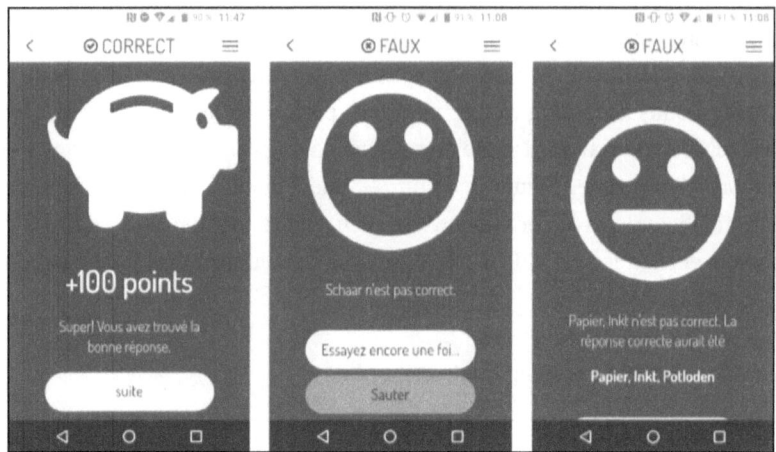

On D-day, the psTs were present in the rooms they were in charge of and welcomed the pupils as they circulated in the museum with their games. The control group performed the hunt on paper and the test group played the game on the mobile app. The pupils from the test group had tested the app with a mini bound game right before coming to the museum, simply to familiarize themselves with the basic features of the app on a tablet.

At the end of the activity, the psTs were asked to fill in a questionnaire to collect their opinions/impressions on the activity and the use of digital technology. The researchers also held a follow-up focus group to further refine the results of the questionnaires.

This data enabled us to draw up the digital profiles of each of the psTs based on Niess et al.'s (2009) Technological Pedagogical Content Knowledge (TPACK) developmental model[9], thereby situating them in the digital integration process, and more precisely in the integration of Actionbound. The digital profiles found are presented in Figure 5 below.

---

9. See Mishra and Koehler (2006) for a presentation of TPACK.

Figure 5. Digital profiles of the ten psTs[10] based on Niess et al.'s (2009, p. 10) TPACK developmental model

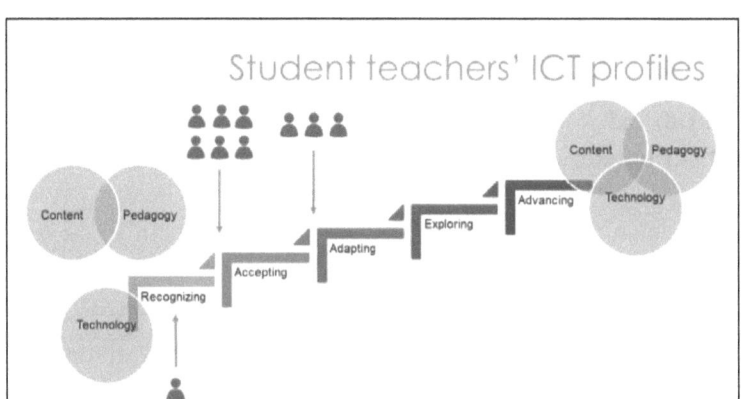

One psT is at the recognizing stage. In sum, it is a stage of alignment of technology with content where the person is neither in favor nor against technology, has no intention of using the technology, thinks that technology is not easy to use for pupils, but that it can complement traditional teaching. Six psTs are situated in-between the recognizing/accepting stages, viz. an alignment of technology with content to motivate students, but with no real pedagogical integration. At that stage people are in favor of the use of technology but do not perceive the pedagogical added value of the tool (technology is simply a substitution option); they view technology as a complement to traditional teaching and believe it is important to use technology adequately. Three psTs are in-between the accepting/adapting stages, meaning that they are in favor of the use of technology, are ready to integrate technology in activities, and clearly see the pedagogical added value. The two research questions that we had for our target population (psTs) were the following ones:

> RQ1. Does the use of Actionbound [along with the pedagogical support of the research team] raise the psTs' awareness regarding the concept of image rights?

---
10. Only ten out of the 11 psTs answered the questionnaire.

# Chapter 12

RQ2. Does the use of Actionbound [along with the pedagogical support from the research team] raise the psTs' awareness regarding the concept of OERs?

These questions were briefly addressed in CALL 2018 proceedings (Meurice et al., 2018) and will be tackled here in more detail. Figure 6 below depicts the psTs' perceptions on image rights therefore addressing our first research question.

Figure 6. psTs' perceptions on image rights

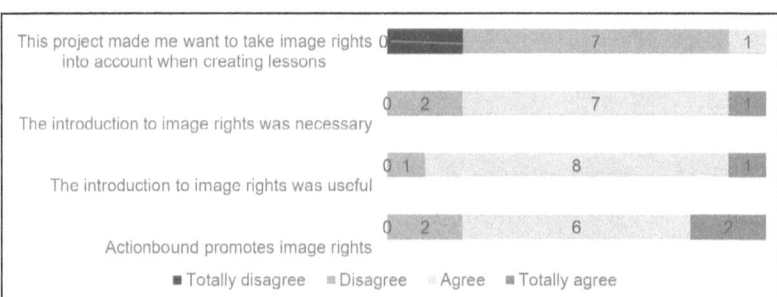

The results do not seem to indicate a correlation between awareness (overall agreement in terms of necessity, usefulness, and promotion of image rights) and implementation (overall disagreement in terms of wanting to take image rights into account in the future). This lack of correlation could perhaps be explained by various factors such as the psTs' own experiences as learners, the complexity or the novelty of the concept, or the lack of a collaborative culture among teachers. In addition, the psTs are not yet practicing teachers in charge of their own classrooms and groups of learners, which renders real integration impossible at this stage of their professional development.

Regarding our second RQ – viz. does the use of Actionbound [along with the pedagogical support from the research team] raise the student-teachers' awareness regarding the concept of OERs? – our results show that:

- it is motivating for almost all psTs (nine out of ten) to create a free educational resource;

- two psTs find the creation of this OER activity 'normal', two still consider it 'stressful', and two describe it as 'fun' and 'innovative'; and

- psTs have a more consumer-oriented approach than a producer-oriented one: whilst eight out of ten are inclined to use OERs created by other people, only five would agree to create an OER and share it with a community of teachers.

In sum, whilst the concept of OERs was unknown to the psTs at the beginning of the project, these results show a positive evolution on the issue, despite the tendency to adopt a consumer approach to OERs rather than a producer perspective.

## 4. Conclusions

As a reminder, our initial aims for the group of psTs involved in the case study were the following ones:

- to promote the use of mobile and classroom OEPs for L2 reading;

- to foster the development of pre- and in-service teachers' and learners' digital literacy skills, including among others the co-construction of OERs and reflective practices on image rights; and

- to create a local professional learning community and community of practice.

The results of the experiment (see Section 3 above) have shown that the setup of our study has come some way to meeting our first aim. It would indeed be necessary to carry out further activities and/or experiment with the psTs to foster further promotion.

As for our second aim, we believe that the experiment has contributed to the development of the psTs' digital literacy skills but that, as could be expected at that stage of their professional development, there is still room for progress, as shown by the display of ICT profiles in Figure 5.

Regarding our third aim, a one-off experiment is certainly not sufficient to create a solid community of practice, but case studies like ours constitute initial steps that have to be taken towards that goal. Teacher trainers should set an example in fostering the development of PLCs including the various types of actors listed in R. Ellis's (2009) Second Language Acquisition (SLA) – language pedagogy nexus, viz. SLA researchers, classroom researchers, teacher educators, and language teachers. Relying on teachers' experience to foster reflexive discussions (Buysse, Sparkman, & Wesley, 2003) is essential and PLCs have been found to have strong potential for change in the professional culture of a school and for an actual fundamental shift in the habits of mind that teachers bring to their daily work in the classroom (see Vescio, Ross, & Adams, 2008 analysis of 11 studies on PLC). To quote Mercieca (2017) in her excellent discussion of communities of practice, "this form of social learning, as described by Bandura (1977), is particularly relevant to the higher education sector in the light of contemporary change and upheaval in society and the university world" (p. 3). This is especially true in practice-based programs in higher education institutions, as we have to ensure that, to quote Mercieca (2017) again, students "are supported to successfully negotiate the change in identity" (p. 9) involved in the professional learning path. Taking part in PLC and being active in professional communities of practice thus seem essential for all stakeholders in education.

## Acknowledgements

We would like to warmly thank our colleagues Carole Delforge and Nathalie Delvigne for their invaluable help in carrying out the experiment and in analyzing the results. We also want to thank the psTs, the pupils, and their classroom teacher who took part in the experiment. Finally we would like to thank the Hergé Museum for their interest and collaboration throughout the project. This experiment was made possible thanks to the governmental funding received for the Consortium Langues Modernes, as part of the overall Pacte pour un Enseignement d'Excellence project.

## Supplementary materials

https://research-publishing.box.com/s/lnr7ltb64gced3stzhnfvlq5yg7cea1p

## References

Bandura, A. (1977). *Social learning theory*. Prentice Hall.

Bliss, T., Robinson, T., Hilton, J., & Wiley, D. (2013). An OER COUP: college teacher and student perceptions of open educational resources. *Journal of Interactive Media in Education, 1*, 1-25. https://doi.org/10.5334/2013-04

Buysse, V., Sparkman, K. L., & Wesley, P. W. (2003). Communities of practice: connecting what we know with what we do. *Exceptional Children, 69*(3), 263-277. https://doi.org/10.1177/001440290306900301

Carretero, S., Vuorikari, R., & Punie, Y. (2017). *DigComp 2.1: the digital competence framework for citizens with eight proficiency levels and examples of use* (No. JRC106281). Joint Research Centre (Seville site).

Ellis, R. (2009). Second language acquisition, teacher education and language pedagogy. *Language Teaching, 43*(2), 182-201. https://doi.org/10.1017/S0261444809990139

Lebrun, M., Lison, C., & Batier, C. (2016). The effects of technopedagogical support for teachers on their pedagogical options, practices and attitudes professional development. *International Journal of Higher Education Pedagogy, 32*(1). http://journals.openedition.org/ripes/1028

Mercieca, B. (2017). What is a community of practice? In J. MacDonald & A. Cater-Steel (Eds), *Communities of Practice* (pp. 3-25). Springer. https://doi.org/10.1007/978-981-10-2879-3_1

Meurice, A. (2018). *The TELLOP online training programme an analysis of the trainees' perception of the French-speaking module*. Master's dissertation. UCLouvain, Louvain-la-Neuve. http://hdl.handle.net/2078.1/thesis:14167

Meurice, A., Van de Vyver, J., Meunier, F., & Delforge, C. (2018). Open your data: digital literacies and language learning through the mobile app Actionbound. In *CALL your DATA, Proceedings, Brugge, KULeuven & imec, 4 - 6 July 2018*. https://www.call2018.org/wp-content/uploads/2018/07/proceedings-CALL-2018.pdf

Mishra, P., & Koehler, M. J. (2006). Technological pedagogical content knowledge: a framework for teacher knowledge. *Teachers College Record, 108*(6), 1017-1054. https://doi.org/10.5944/openpraxis.8.1.236

Mishra, S., Sharma, M., Sharma, R., Singh, A., & Thakur, A. (2016). Development of a scale to measure faculty attitude towards open educational resources. *Open Praxis, 8*(1), 55-69. https://doi.org/10.5944/openpraxis.8.1.236

Niess, M. L., Ronau, R. N., Shafer, K. G., Driskell, S. O., Harper S., Johnston, C., Browning, C., Ozgun-Koca, S. A., & Kersaint, G. (2009). Mathematics teacher TPACK standards and development model. *Contemporary Issues in Technology and Teacher Education, 9*(1), 4-24.

Pérez-Paredes, P., Ordoñana Guillamón, C., & Aguado Jiménez, P. (2018). Language teachers' perceptions on the use of OER language processing technologies in MALL. *Computer Assisted Language Learning, 31*(5-6), 1-24. https://doi.org/10.1080/09588221.2017.1418754

Puentedura, R. (2013). *SAMR: moving from enhancement to transformation*. Paper presented at AIS ICT Management and Leadership Conference, Canberra. http://www.hippasus.com/rrpweblog/archives/2013/05/29/SAMREnhancementToTransformation.pdf

Rolfe, V. (2012). Open educational resources: staff attitudes and awareness. *Research in Learning Technology, 20*, 1-13.

Sabadie, J., Muñoz, J., Punie, Y., Redecker, C., & Vuorikari, R. (2014). OER: a European policy perspective. *Journal of Interactive Media in Education*, 1-12. https://doi.org/10.5334/2014-05

UNESCO. (n.d.). *Open educational resources | United Nations educational, scientific and cultural organization*. http://www.unesco.org/new/en/communication-and-information/access-to-knowledge/open-educational-resources/xx

Vescio, V., Ross, D., & Adams, A. (2008). A review of research on the impact of professional learning communities on teaching practice and student learning, *Teaching and teacher education, 24*(1), 80-91. https://doi.org/10.1016/j.tate.2007.01.004

# 13. Exploratory practice: a way of opening up access to research by classroom teachers and learners

## Assia Slimani-Rolls[1]

### Abstract

Engaging in research is acknowledged as having a potentially transformative impact on the professional development of language teachers (Borg, 2010). Yet a cursory examination of the literature suggests that teachers rarely engage in research. The aim of this chapter is threefold: to introduce Exploratory Practice (EP), a form of inclusive Practitioner Research (PR) designed to empower teachers and their learners to better understand their practice, to illustrate, through a case study, how EP works in the classroom, and finally to report on the recent developments of opening up access and possibilities for language teachers to engage in and make their research public while, at the same time, creating opportunities for themselves to continue with their professional development.

Keywords: exploratory practice, inclusive practitioner research, collegiality, research sustainability, continuing professional development.

---

1. Regent's University London, London, England; rollsa@regents.ac.uk; https://orcid.org/0000-0003-4136-1462

How to cite this chapter: Slimani-Rolls, A. (2019). Exploratory practice: a way of opening up access to research by classroom teachers and learners. In A. Comas-Quinn, A. Beaven & B. Sawhill (Eds), *New case studies of openness in and beyond the language classroom* (pp. 187-198). Research-publishing.net. https://doi.org/10.14705/rpnet.2019.37.975

Chapter 13

## 1. Context of the project

### 1.1. Background of EP

The lack of engagement in research by language teachers has been noted by many scholars in English Language Teaching (ELT) (Borg, 2010) and in Modern Foreign Language (MFL) teaching (Marsden & Kasprowicz, 2017). The barriers preventing this engagement cover a large spectrum of obstacles, many of which are summarised in Borg (2010, p. 409). Suffice it to say, for the needs of this chapter, that a lack of time, research skills, support, and access to theory and research are most notable.

It remains, however, relevant for teachers to engage in research in order to contest their tacit understanding and ensure that their classroom practice is not based only on intuition and experience. In this respect, the eclecticism that characterises teachers' methodologies and the 'sense of plausibility' (Prahbu, 1992) that guides their decision-making processes acknowledges them as reflective practitioners capable of developing their practice. At the same time, it falls upon them to rise to the challenge of showing that they are not mere consumers of academic research and implementers of other people's ideas. They can engage in research to enable themselves to understand the specific and contextual environment in which they operate so they can explain to others what works in their practice, what does not work, and why.

### 1.2. The principled framework of EP

It is essential to realise that teachers cannot undertake research in the same way academic researchers do because their training and working conditions differ drastically. EP has put forward a principled framework (Allwright, 2003) to empower teachers and their learners to understand better their practice by investigating teaching puzzles, such as *why do my students make disruptive use of mobile phones during my lessons?*, as Lecumberri's (2018) study illustrates below. EP believes that asking 'why' instead of 'what' questions leads to a deeper understanding of complex issues rather than finding solutions which may work in some circumstances but not in others (for more teacher and learner puzzles see Allwright, 2003; Allwright & Hanks, 2009; Dikilitas & Hanks, 2018; Slimani-Rolls & Kiely, 2018). EP is part of the PR family which includes, amongst others, reflective practice (Farrell, 2008), action research (Burns, 2005), and exploratory action research (Smith, Connelly, & Rebolledo, 2014). As in any family, differences between siblings exist and EP differentiates itself by a number of distinctive principles which characterise its theoretical framework as listed and explained below.

## 1.3. Principles of EP

- Quality of life for language teachers and learners is the most appropriate central concern for EP.

- Working primarily to understand the quality of life, as it is experienced by language learners and teachers, is more important than, and logically prior to, seeking in any way to improve it.

- Everybody needs to be involved in the work for understanding.

- The work needs to serve to bring people together.

- The work needs to be conducted in a spirit of mutual development.

- Working for understanding is necessarily a continuous enterprise.

- Integrating the work for understanding fully into existing curricular practices is a way of minimising the burden and maximising sustainability (Allwright & Hanks, 2009, pp. 149-154)

Quality of life is prioritised in the classroom because it is believed that it is the search for quality of life that paves the way to quality of work. When teachers and learners feel respected, listened to, and enjoy rather than endure their classroom experiences, then they invest their efforts in developing the quality of their work.

Seeking to understand quality of life should come before attempting to bring any change because understanding is "a prerequisite to intelligent decision-making" (Allwright & Hanks, 2009, p. 151).

The principles of collegiality and inclusivity for mutual development are crucial to embed in the research enterprise. Indeed, it is imperative that all those involved in the research are given the opportunity to contribute with their ideas and, by the same token, derive a positive learning experience. In particular, inclusivity of learners as co-partners is essential as EP suggests that learners are an integral part of the classroom environment and that their involvement in the search for its understanding is paramount. In order to make sense of their practice without getting burnt out, EP recommends that teachers integrate the search for understanding into their teaching routine so that both, teaching and research, get done at the same time. For this purpose, EP proposes that teachers use normal classroom activities as research tools to investigate the teaching puzzles. These activities can include brainstorming sessions, class discussion, pair/group work, reading comprehension texts, surveys, video recording, and any other pedagogic activity that teachers find suitable. Developing expertise in using the tools of their trade as investigative instruments would make the teachers' search for understanding feasible and sustainable.

## 2. Intended outcomes

The investigation of *why do my students make disruptive use of mobile phones during my lessons?* was carried out by Lecumberri (2018) within a larger project (Slimani-Rolls & Kiely, 2018) whose aim was to encourage language teachers, in my own institution, to use EP in their normal classroom environment, as advocated by its proponents. For this purpose, I invited practitioners teaching languages for business purposes to undergraduate students to join our two year long project. Three English and three MFL teachers (French, Italian, and Spanish) volunteered. They were four females and two males, each of whom had ten to over 15 years of teaching experience. Five had an MA in applied linguistics and one a diploma in teaching.

Prior to the start of the project, I introduced EP to the participating teachers to enable them to come up with their respective puzzle. Subsequently, we discussed together the research programme which would help them to scaffold their investigative efforts. Three strategies emerged: First, I recommended that the teachers use the existing institutional peer observation of teaching scheme to engage with each other. The resulting conversations about their teaching would allow them to refine their thinking about the puzzle area by reflecting upon it and further discussing it with colleagues. EP stresses that teachers focus on putting the puzzle area into a question starting with 'why', seeking for deep understanding rather than using 'what', which might bring up an ephemeral solution. However, it soon became apparent that identifying a puzzle was not problematic to the participating teachers. Second, some of them requested access to support in case they encountered issues with their investigations, as for most of them, their research experience was limited to the MA dissertation that they undertook many years ago. Hence, I made myself available as a mentor and offered individual consultations to support their research initiatives. The mentoring process provided guidance on EP principles and technical aspects of research design and practice. It also instilled encouragement and confidence building so they could take their puzzle investigation forward. However, the teachers clearly remained at the heart of this process-oriented project as they were working on their own agenda rather than following a pre-established schedule. Third, we agreed to meet together, once every six weeks, to share and discuss the questions, apprehensions, understandings, and misunderstandings about the teaching puzzles within the supportive professional community that we had built up.

## 3. Nuts and bolts

### 3.1. The activity

Esther Lecumberri is a teacher of Spanish and one of the six participating teachers (Lecumberri, 2018). She explained that one of her teaching groups was particularly challenging as the students seemed demotivated and tended to make excessive use of their mobile phones, thus, marring the quality of life in the classroom. On the one hand, Lecumberri (2018) was aware of the institutional ban on the use of these devices, but she was also aware that they can be employed usefully as dictionaries, cameras, recorders, and information providers. Hence, for the benefit of the students, she refused to ban them indiscriminately. On the other hand, she was frustrated by the disruptive use that the students made of their mobiles. So, she decided to raise this puzzling issue with the students in a class discussion. As their language level was intermediate, Lecumberri (2018) seized this opportunity for them to practise their Spanish. Although she was surprised by their vehement rejection that mobile phones could impact negatively in the class, she was pleased with the level of involvement that the students showed during the discussion. They said that they felt respected and treated like adults, defending the view that they were using mobiles sensibly.

Subsequently, Lecumberri (2018) video recorded, with the students' permission, one of their classroom events hoping to demonstrate the disruption that not all the students had, so far, acknowledged in order to make them understand her frustration and negotiate a change of attitude. Once she felt that they were ready for another discussion, she asked them to view the video in groups with the task of assessing the level of disruption that they could see and hear. The groups reported, in Spanish, that particular instances were clearly disruptive, and some assured that it was ultimately the teacher's responsibility to monitor the level of mobile use intrusion.

Furthermore, Lecumberri (2018) followed the students' comments by developing a short survey with questions related to the impact that mobile phones could have on (1) their concentration and participation, (2) the use of the university policy, and (3) the classroom participants' responsibility in restricting the use of these devices. She distributed the survey for the students to fill out, discuss their responses in groups, and then report the content of their discussion to the whole class. It emerged that the students recognised that the assumption that they could attend to the classroom interaction and, at the same time, respond to their acquaintances was not necessarily tenable. They also understood the frustration that this behaviour could cause to the teacher and their peers and admitted that protecting the classroom quality of life was not only the teacher's but everybody's responsibility.

## 3.2. Reflection and interpretation

Lecumberri (2018) explained that adopting an inclusive approach of listening and negotiating rather than imposing her authority to restrict mobile phone use enabled her to enhance, rather than damage, her relationship with the students which, she believes, is essential for the quality of classroom life. Opening up communication channels for meaningful exchanges between herself and the students and between the students themselves allowed the classroom participants to understand what it is that they are trying to achieve together. Lecumberri (2018) noted that

> "the benefit [derived from using EP] is initially improved communication processes which, in turn, enhances the relationship between the teacher and the learners and facilitates effective teaching and learning activities and participation" (p. 117).

## 3.3. Implications

As the use of mobile phones was endemic in her other classes and those of her colleagues, Lecumberri (2018) opted to tackle this puzzle with the rest of her classes and share her EP knowledge with colleagues across the institution in order to construct more academically oriented use of mobiles. Ester felt that she had not only regained confidence in her own classroom management skills, but she has also gained respect for the learners who collaborated with her to build a more conducive environment for learning.

While the above step-by-step methodological account of Lecumberri's (2018) investigation puzzle may be helpful to get neophyte EP practitioners started, it is worth noting that the steps are not intended as a rigid prescription. Rather, what is central to EP enquiries are the EP principles because they serve to create the context which facilitates the search for understanding by teachers. Once they get to be more conversant with EP, teachers become more creative about developing, together with their learners, EP strategies for investigating their classroom environment.

It is important to realise that a chronological sequence is not intended by the order in which Lecumberri's (2018) investigative processes have been presented. The first set of EP processes taken up by Lecumberri (2018) above are:

- **taking action for understanding by focussing on the processes themselves** such as making herself aware of puzzling issues of classroom life; thinking harder with other practitioners (learners, peers, and mentors) inside (and/or outside) the classroom; looking/listening and attending more intensively to what is going on, as it is going on in the classroom; and planning for understanding by adopting familiar pedagogic procedures (class/group discussion and video recording/ survey) to help her develop participant understanding. These are indeed interrelated processes and often concurrent with the next set of processes;

- **working with emerging understanding by focussing on the content of the processes** such as reflexively expressing and appraising personal/ collective insights; refining notions of potential 'change' if necessary as planned by the teacher; discussing potential personal or collective moves; sharing personal understandings of processes as a way of supporting others and of inviting others to join the EP community of practice as Lecumberri (2018) has done with her various teaching groups and subsequently with her own colleagues to professionalise her practice.

At this point, it is important to highlight the various and thriving means of opening up access to EP and PR in general. They encourage, as illustrated below, teachers' ownership to develop their own community of practice to use, revise, redistribute and remix creative works that are shared by teachers across the world (Wiley, 2014).

## 4. Conclusion

Bridging the gap between research and practice is essential and so efforts are made to motivate teachers to work towards understanding their practice. A number of resources are available to open up access to engagement in research. These include Instruments for Research into Second Languages (IRIS)[2], a digital repository of data collection materials developed to facilitate access to PR (Thompson, Marsden, & Plonsky, 2018). Amongst the many uses of IRIS, teachers are directed towards methodologies to allow them to investigate issues directly relevant to their classroom environment, for instance: "why are my students sometimes unwilling to communicate in class? How do my learners feel about learning English? Why are my learners studying English? What motivates them? Are the materials I use communicative enough?" (Thompson et al., 2018, p. 79). IRIS materials link to Open Accessible Summaries In Language Studies (OASIS)[3], which supplies summaries of journal articles to facilitate teachers' search for information which can then be downloaded. IRIS can be followed on Facebook[4] for updates on new materials and for news on open science.

Carrying out and publishing their own research is something that teachers are simply not familiar with. In this respect, Bullock and Smith (2015) ask "why should teachers have to change their 'day jobs' to share what they know?" (p. 77). They draw attention to blogging, tweeting, and posting in social networks as possible alternatives for opening up more appealing and user-friendly genres for teachers to disseminate their work. As Kahle (2008) explains, "[o]penness is measured by the degree to which it empowers users to take action making technology [and content] their own, rather than imposing its own foreign and inflexible requirements and constraints" (p. 35). Along these lines of thinking, the teacher research Special Interest Group (SIG) of the International Association of Teachers of English as a Foreign Language

---

2. www.iris-database.org

3. www.oasis-database.org

4. https://www.facebook.com/irisdatabase/

Chapter 13

(henceforth IATEFL Research SIG) is currently playing a leading role in demystifying research by enabling teachers to initiate and carry out research that is relevant to them and share their outcomes in ways that suit them.

The IATEFL Research SIG organises a one day Pre-Conference Event (PCE) devoted to PR by and for teachers. Rather than using formal papers presented by teachers standing on a podium, the PCE invites teachers to talk in front of their poster for up to five minutes before and after a morning coffee break. This gallery style format frees up ample time for delegates and presenters to join in the participatory nature of the event and discuss the content of the posters. The afternoon is generally taken up with the participants sharing their views about and experiences with PR including spontaneous commentaries rather than prepared speeches by experts such as Allwright, Burns, and Freeman so that the focus remains on the participants' own experiences. The presentations are subsequently published in a free e-book entitled *Teachers Research!*, with an exclamation mark stressing that teachers do indeed carry out research when appropriate development models, such as EP, are made accessible. Like the present volume, this book offers a less intimidating way of reporting on research activities in creative and varied writing styles and use of visuals with a practical orientation. It also includes the hyperlinks to website-based video-recordings and posters. The book *Teachers Research!* was nominated for a British Council ELTons award (innovation in teacher resources) in 2016 and was said to be "[a]n interesting, varied collection of research stories, which should inspire and give confidence to teachers to pursue their own research" (IATEFL, n.d., n.p.).

The emerging dissemination genres of research for and by teachers seen above are not limited to the PCE event in the UK. They have become a regular format in the efforts of IATEFL Research SIG and the British Council to open up PR in Europe, India, and Latin America. The *Teachers Research!* Chile 2016 conference attracted 120 participants with presenters from Argentina, Brazil, Colombia, and Uruguay; the Buenos Aires *Teachers Research!* 2017 conference and Istanbul *Teachers Research!* 2017 conference highlight the popularity of these events and testify to the growing interest that is shown by academics, professional bodies, and teachers themselves to develop PR that is central to their professional development.

## References

Allwright, D. (2003). A brief guide to 'Exploratory Practice: Rethinking practitioners research in language teaching'. *Language Teaching Research, 7*(2), 109-111. https://doi.org/10.1191/1362168803lr117oa

Allwright, D., & Hanks, J. (2009). *The developing language learner. An introduction to exploratory practice*. Palgrave Macmillan

Borg, S. (2010). Language teacher research engagement. *Language Teaching, 43*(4), 391-429. https://doi.org/10.1017/s0261444810000170

Bullock, D., & Smith, R. (Eds). (2015). *Teacher research!* IATEFL.

Burns, A. (2005). Action research: an evolving paradigm. *Language Teaching, 38*(1), 57-74.

Dikilitas, K., & Hanks, J. (Eds). (2018). *Developing language teachers with exploratory practice. Innovations and explorations in language education.* Palgrave Macmillan. https://doi.org/10.1007/978-3-319-75735-3_1

Farrell, T. S. C. (2008). *Reflecting language teaching: from research to practice.* Continuum Press.

IATEFL. (n.d.). *Teachers research!* IATEFL Research SIG. http://resig.weebly.com/teachers-research.html

Kahle, D. (2008). Designing open education technology. In T. Liyoshi & M. S. V. Kumar (Eds), *Opening up education* (pp. 27-45). MIT Press.

Lecumberri, M. E. (2018). Mobile phones in my language classroom: a cause for concern or a source of communication. In A. Slimani-Rolls & R. Kiely, *Exploratory practice for continuing professional development. An innovative approach for language teachers.* Palgrave Macmillan. https://doi.org/10.1007/978-3-319-69763-5_6

Marsden, E., & Kasprowicz, R. (2017). Foreign language educators' exposure to research: reported experiences, exposure via citations, and a proposal for action. *The Modern Language Journal, 104*(4), 613-642. https://doi.org/10.1111/modl.12426

Prahbu, N. S. (1992). The dynamics of the language lesson. *TESOL Quarterly, 26*(2), 225-242.

Slimani-Rolls, A., & Kiely, R. (Eds). (2018). *Exploratory practice for continuing professional development. An innovative approach for language teachers.* Palgrave Macmillan.

Smith, R. (2015). The concept, and spirit of teachers research! In D. Bullock & R. Smith (Eds), *Teacher research!* IATEFL.

Smith, R., Connelly, T., & Rebolledo, P. (2014). Teacher-research as continuing professional development: a project with Chilean secondary school teachers. In D. Hayes (Ed.), *Innovations in the continuing professional development of English language teachers.* British Council.

Thompson, S., Marsden, E., & Plonsky, L. (2018). Facilitating teacher research using IRIS: a digital repository of instruments used for research in second languages. In J. Mackay, M. Birello & D. Xerri (Eds), *ELT research in action: bridging the gap between research & classroom practice.* IATEFL.

Wiley, D. (2014, March 5). *The access compromise and the 5th R.* http://opencontent.org/blog/archives/3221

# Author index

**B**
Beaven, Ana  v, 1
Beaven, Tita  x, 5, 145
Berti, Margherita  x, 3, 37
Blyth, Carl S.  ix, xvii
Boykova, Natalia  x, 4, 65

**C**
Campbell, Lorna  x, 4, 85
Comas-Quinn, Anna  v, 1, 4, 101
Conde Gafaro, Barbara  x, 5, 115

**D**
Daniels, Patricia  xi, 5, 159
Durán Urrea, Evelyn  xi, 3, 23

**F**
Fuertes Gutiérrez, Mara  xi, 4, 101

**G**
Gabaudan, Odette  xi, 4, 49
Godwin-Jones, Robert  xi, 4, 65

**K**
Kelly, Olivia  xii, 5, 129

**M**
Mathieu, Lionel  xii, 4, 65
McAndrew, Ewan  xii, 4, 85
Meiners, Jocelly G.  xii, 3, 23
Meunier, Fanny  xiii, 6, 173
Meurice, Alice  xiii, 6, 173
Middlebrooks, Laura  xiii, 4, 65
Murphy-Judy, Kathryn  xiii, 4, 65

**N**
Nocchi, Susanna  xiii, 4, 49

**P**
Pio, Carlos  xiv, 3, 11

**S**
Sawhill, Barbara  v, 1
Slimani-Rolls, Assia  xiv, 6, 187

**V**
Van de Vyver, Julie  xiv, 6, 173
Viana da Silva, Eduardo  xv, 3, 11

www.ingramcontent.com/pod-product-compliance
Lightning Source LLC
Chambersburg PA
CBHW022007160426
43197CB00007B/319